YORK NOTES

General Editors: Professor A.N. Je
of Stirling) & Professor Suheil Bush
University of Beirut)

Laurie Lee

CIDER WITH ROSIE

Notes by Jean Tobin

MA PH D (WISCONSIN)
Associate Professor, University of Wisconsin Center in Sheboygan

LONGMAN
YORK PRESS

Extracts from *Cider with Rosie* by Laurie Lee are reprinted by kind permission of the author and The Hogarth Press.

YORK PRESS
Immeuble Esseily, Place Riad Solh, Beirut

LONGMAN GROUP UK LIMITED
Longman House, Burnt Mill, Harlow,
Essex CM20 2JE, England
Associated companies, branches and representatives
throughout the world

First published 1982
Seventh impression 1993

ISBN 0-582-03365-9

Printed in Hong Kong
WLEE/04

Contents

Part 1

Introduction

The author's life and works

Laurie Lee, poet, dramatist, essayist, and writer of memoirs, was born on 26 June 1914, in the English town of Stroud, Gloucestershire. A sickly infant, as he cheerfully mentions in *Cider with Rosie*, he was once almost laid out for burial by mistake. In England in the early years of the twentieth century, no one expected that all the children in a family would survive; in Lee's family four of his father's twelve children died, and one was sent to live with a grandmother. Thus Lee's mother was in charge of seven children when, to use his phrase, his father 'skipped to London', and the family moved from Stroud to a small village up the valley.

Lee attended Slad Village School and later Stroud Central School; he finished his formal education at fifteen. Much more important to him than his indifferent schooling were his poetry and music. He played his violin at village celebrations for the next few years, and when he left the village, he supported himself on the road by playing his violin for pennies. First he tramped to the sea and along the English coast, learning much from men set wandering by the widespread unemployment of the nineteen-thirties. He then walked to London and worked there as a builder's labourer for a full year before purchasing a one-way ticket on a boat sailing for Spain. He landed in Vigo with a blanket, a knapsack, and his violin; in the thirteen months left before the outbreak of the Spanish Civil War, Lee walked to Zamora, Toro, Valladolid, Segovia, Madrid, Toledo, Cadiz, Seville, Algeciras, and Castillo.

An abrupt end to his adventures came when he was taken from the coast of southern Spain by the British Navy, and he returned home in a ship sent to pick up British citizens stranded by war. He stayed in England only a short time, however, before returning to Spain to fight, 'crossing the Pyrenees', he writes, 'in the winter of 1937 to find that the war was already lost'. During the few years left before the outbreak of the Second World War, he was a wanderer, travelling, in his own words, 'round the Eastern Mediterranean as an odd-job tramp, visiting Italy, Greece, the Aegean Islands, and spending a winter in Cyprus'.

Since 1944, Lee has lived as a professional writer, serving as publications editor at the Ministry of Information from 1944 to 1946, and writing documentary film-scripts for the Crown Film Unit from 1946 to 1947. In 1947 he published a verse play, *Peasant's Priest*, and in 1948 wrote *The Voyage of Magellan*, a play for radio. From 1950 to 1951, he wrote for the Festival of Britain, and in 1951 he was given a Society of Authors' Travelling Scholarship.

In 1944, Lee had published his first book of poems, *The Sun My Monument*. His second book of poems, *The Bloom of Candles*, won an Atlantic Award in 1947; his third, *My Many-Coated Man*, won the Foyle Poetry Award and was chosen by the 1953 Poetry Book Society. Lee's prose works were also well received: when *Cider with Rosie* was published by The Hogarth Press in England in 1959, it was awarded the W. H. Smith £1,000 Award for Literature and was a Book Society Choice; in 1960, when the work was published in the United States under the title *The Edge of Day*, it was chosen by the Book of the Month Club.

Cider with Rosie is the first of two autobiographical books by Laurie Lee. It describes his boyhood in a Gloucestershire village in the west of England. *As I Walked Out One Midsummer Morning* (1969) is the second autobiographical book. Beginning with the day Lee left the village as a very young man, it describes his travels of the next several years as Lee walked to the sea, to London, and then through Spain. Other brief periods in Lee's life are presented in *A Rose for Winter* (1955), a travel book about a three-month return to southern Spain many years later, and in *I Can't Stay Long* (1975). Lee's wife—the beautiful Kati from Provence—appears in *A Rose for Winter*; Lee's daughter, Jesse Frances, born in 1962, is the subject of 'The Firstborn', one of the essays collected in *I Can't Stay Long*. In 'Writing Autobiography', also collected in *I Can't Stay Long*; Lee states, 'In common with other writers I have written little that was not for the most part autobiographical.'

Historical background

In the chapter entitled 'Village School' in *Cider with Rosie* Lee states that the children learned 'a few mnemonics, a jumbled list of wars, and a dreamy image of the world's geography' (p. 42*); from his readers, Lee requires a little more. *Cider with Rosie* begins in June 1918, during the last year of the First World War. That year, David Lloyd George (1863–1945) was Prime Minister; George V (1865–1936) had been on the British throne since 1910; George's predecessor had been his father, Edward VII (1841–1910); Edward's mother Victoria

*All page references in these Notes are to the Penguin edition of *Cider with Rosie*, Penguin Books, Harmöndsworth, 1962.

had ruled between 1837 and 1901. Victoria, married to her beloved Albert in 1840, had seen him named Prince Consort in 1857, four years before his death. Thus, even though in 'Village School', young Laurie dutifully chants with the rest, 'One-King-is-George. One-George-is-Fifth. . . .' (p. 53), within a few pages he has not only confused kings and consorts, but faltered and fallen two monarchs behind. In 'The Kitchen', in response to the brotherly challenge, 'What's the name of the king, then?', he quietly mutters, 'Albert' (p. 65).

In *Cider with Rosie*, Lee mentions three of Britain's wars: the Boer War (1899–1902), the First World War (1914–18), and the Second World War (1939–45). The first two of these had made heroes of young Laurie's uncles. Uncle Sid and Uncle Charlie both fought in the South African War, or Boer War (named after African settlers of Dutch descent, the Boers), which had been declared against Great Britain by the independent Transvaal and the Orange Free State in October 1899, after the British had sent troops into the area to protect their commercial interests. The war ended in May 1902, with the Treaty of Vereeniging. As a result of the British victory, the Boer territories were annexed and the Union of South Africa was formed. Recounting some of his Uncle Charlie's stories, Lee briefly describes the rough-and-tumble life in South Africa immediately after the war (pp. 171–2).

Several more of Lee's uncles—all five of the Light brothers—were soldiers in the First World War, and Lee's memories of being three years old include that Great War: 'All my life was the war, and the war was the world' (p. 21). Most particularly, Lee recalls the war's end: the spontaneous bonfires the night the news came (pp. 21–4), the parade in costume on Peace Day (pp. 184–7), and the way the village later 'filled up with unknown men who stood around in their braces and khaki pants, smoking short pipes . . . and gazing in silence at the gardens' (p. 25). During the First World War the uncles came home on leave to sleep 'like the dead all day' (p. 169); during the Second World War, it was Lee himself who similarly came home only to fall into an exhausted sleep (p. 134). Never in *Cider with Rosie* does Lee mention political or military aspects to distinguish any of these three specific wars. He recalls that the village store gave out bags of prunes in celebration, not that the First World War ended when the armistice was signed at Compiègne on 11 November 1918. If anything, Lee's commentary stresses the continuity between wars. All exhausted soldiers are alike, he seems to suggest; the five uncles are deliberately compared to the Roman soldiers who fought under Caesar (p. 183).

Lee also stresses the continuity in village life. The focus of his book is here, on a way of life unchanged for centuries, the daily pace still set by the limits of the horse as in the time of Caesar. Historical accident jolted Lee out of the easy unawareness derived from a habitual way of life: 'I belonged', Lee writes, 'to that generation which saw, by chance, the end of a thousand years' life' (p. 216). What happened in the village happened throughout Great Britain. 'In or about December, 1910, human character changed', asserted Virginia Woolf (1882–1941) in that famous essay called 'Mr Bennett and Mrs Brown'; she added that there had occurred 'at the same time a change in religion, conduct, politics, and literature'.* In the small distant villages, the transformation—no less complete when it came than in London—was postponed for a few years. 'The change', writes Lee, 'came late to our Cotswold valley, didn't really show itself till the late 1920s' (p. 216).

Apparently the so-called Industrial Revolution, which transformed much of the British countryside between 1750 and 1850, had largely bypassed the village and left its social fabric complete. That 'revolution' marked the shift from hand tools to machines, from an agricultural and commercial society to a modern industrial one. Its traces are present in *Cider with Rosie*: in 'The Kitchen', for example, Lee's half-sister Dorothy goes off to work 'in a decayed cloth-mill by a stream', and Lee casually describes the early hour 'when walkers and bicyclists flowed down the long hills to Stroud, when the hooters called through the morning dews and factories puffed out their plumes' (p. 68). However, Lee shows many other villagers earning their livelihoods by less modern, even feudal, means. In addition to working 'down in the cloth-mills at Stroud', he says, the chief ways of making a living in the village were working 'on the farms' and 'working for the Squire' (p. 42).

In contrast, from the late 1920s onwards, the 'change' was overwhelming in the Cotswolds villages. The advent of modern technology brought the motor-car, charabanc, motor-bike, radio, movies—all of which meant the villages would never again be isolated to the same degree as before. Lee, as well as Virginia Woolf, read the new literature; the vicar—perhaps objecting to the novel's frank presentation of sexual matters—tore *Sons and Lovers* (by D. H. Lawrence, 1885–1930) from his hands, but even the church's power was fading. In the elegaic chapter, 'Last Days', Lee records the passing of old feudal relationships: the old Squire died, 'the Big House was sold by auction and became a Home for Invalids. . . . His servants dispersed and went into the factories. His nephew broke up the estate' (p. 222). The social fabric of the village changed for ever.

Lee's awareness of the significance of the 'change' makes his book particularly valuable. More than the autobiography of a single individual, *Cider with Rosie* is a record of an entire village, representative of many such villages; the memories the book preserves are of a long-established way of life, and of its passing.

*Virginia Woolf, *Collected Essays*, vol. I, Harcourt Brace, New York, 1967, pp. 320–1.

General literary background

Cider with Rosie is classified as an autobiography; it is written in prose and is essentially non-fiction. However, the book is reminiscent of many other works, some of which are written in poetry, not prose, and some of which are classified as fiction.

For example, *Cider with Rosie* might remind readers of those works which evoke specific small sections of English countryside. Reading of the Cotswolds of Laurie Lee, one thinks of the Exmoor of Richard D. Blackmore's (1825–1900) historical novel, *Lorna Doone* (1869), or of the Wessex novels of Thomas Hardy (1840–1928), his wild heathlands and the rustics who form a chorus to his tragedies. Again, *Cider with Rosie* is reminiscent of the loving portrayal of the Lake District in William Wordsworth's (1770–1850) long autobiographical poem, *The Prelude; or, The Growth of a Poet's Mind* (1805), particularly Books First and Second, which treat of Wordsworth's childhood: 'I grew up/ . . . Much favoured in my birthplace, and no less/ In that beloved Vale to which ere long/ We were transplanted' (I.301). In the great poet's account of growing up in his own remote village, Hawkshead, there are passages later echoed in *Cider with Rosie*, for in spite of the differences in the locations, simple village pleasures in each were largely the same. Lee's description, for instance, of his family gathered together after supper in 'The Kitchen' (pp. 74–7) recalls Wordsworth's earlier telling of 'home amusements by the warm peat-fire/ at evening' while 'abroad/ Incessant rain was falling, or the frost/ Raged bitterly, with keen and silent tooth' (I.505). Again, the account given by Lee of evening games of Fox and Hounds in 'Winter and Summer' recalls Wordsworth's memories of similar games played in the 1780s: 'Duly were our games/ Prolonged in summer till the day-light failed/ . . . at last,/ When all the ground was dark, and twinkling stars/ Edged the black clouds, home and to bed we went,/ Feverish with weary joints and beating minds' (II.9).

Unchanged for centuries, the village life recalled by Lee may be familiar to readers because they have encountered it in so many early English novels. The position in *Cider with Rosie* of Squire Jones is like that of Squire Allworthy, adopted father of Tom in the novel *Tom Jones* (1749) by Henry Fielding (1707–54). The vicar's duties are relatively unchanged from those of the vicar in *The Vicar of Wakefield* (1766) by Oliver Goldsmith (1728–74). Life in Lee's village is as innocently enjoyable as life in Meryton, described by Jane Austen (1775–1817) in her novel *Pride and Prejudice* (1813); it is as circumscribed, though less genteel, as life in *Middlemarch: A Study of Provincial Life* (1871–2) by George Eliot (1819–80). The viewpoint has shifted, however, even though life in rural England remains the same.

In these eighteenth and nineteenth-century novels, the reader experiences life in the big houses; but, in *Cider with Rosie*, he stands at the outside doors, peering in at the tapestries.

In his last chapter, 'Last Days', Lee records the sudden end of this centuries-old village life: 'Time squared itself, and the village shrank, and distances crept nearer.' Elsewhere in England and the world, the same forces were at work; elsewhere other villagers got into new cars to travel to the next town or reached over to turn on the radio.

In a similar way, many Americans were moved to record village life, evaluate it, and record its passing. Retelling the personal stories of village 'grotesques' in *Winesburg, Ohio* (1919), Sherwood Anderson (1876–1941) revealed the hidden, warping loneliness of village life in the United States. Edgar Lee Masters (1869–1950) allowed his American villagers to speak from the grave of their bitter or fulfilling village lives in *Spoon River Anthology* (1915); they spoke in short unrhymed poems which were inherently dramatic and which recently have been performed on stage. Similarly concerned with the recording and evaluating of provincial life, and even more critical, was Sinclair Lewis (1885–1951), in works such as *Main Street* (1920), about life in Gopher Prairie, Minnesota. In the 1920s, books such as these became common enough in the United States to be grouped under a heading, 'The Revolt from the Village'. Later, a nostalgic and uncritical view of provincial life in Grover's Corners, New Hampshire, was presented in Thornton Wilder's (b. 1897) play, *Our Town* (1938). The British, in general, take a more positive view of village life. *Under Milk Wood: A Play for Voices* (1953) by Dylan Thomas (1914–53) is happily less sentimental than *Our Town*, but still less harsh than *Spoon River Anthology*. The villagers of Llareggub, Thomas's imagined Welsh village, resemble villagers everywhere, including those in Grover's Corners, Spoon River, and Winesburg, Ohio.

One of the most critical of twentieth-century changes in English country life was D. H. Lawrence, who deserves special mention here because Laurie Lee refers to his books in 'Last Days'. Obviously Lee invites comparison between his autobiography and Lawrence's semi-autobiographical novel *Sons and Lovers* (1913) when he describes how the vicar tore that book from young Laurie's hands. Indeed, when Lee recounts the incident in 'True Adventures of the Boy Reader', collected in *I Can't Stay Long*, the confiscated book is Aldous Huxley's (1894–1963) *Brave New World* (1932). Young Laurie might well have identified with Paul Morel, the hero in *Sons and Lovers*; Paul, too, was a boy of great vitality, but sick so often nobody expected him to live through childhood. He and the other children greatly loved their hard-working mother and felt estranged from their father, who abused her. He too aspired to become a poet, and in the last chapter of *Sons and Lovers* prepared to leave his village. The chapter called 'The Young Life of Paul' is probably most like Lee's autobiography; Lawrence's account of being ill, picking blackberries, sharing his mother's delight in flowers, and watching her come home feeling guilty about spending a fivepence on a dish is reminiscent of Lee's young life as he describes it in *Cider with Rosie.*

A note on the text

Unless otherwise specified, page references given in parentheses in these Notes refer to Laurie Lee's *Cider with Rosie*, Penguin Books, Harmondsworth, 1962. In the U.S.A. this edition is published by Viking Penguin, New York. The first edition of *Cider with Rosie* was published by The Hogarth Press, London, in 1959.

Part 2

Summaries
of CIDER WITH ROSIE

A general summary

In *Cider with Rosie*, Laurie Lee recalls his own childhood and adolescence. He was one of seven children in a close family headed by his mother; he grew up in England, in a Cotswold village governed by tradition. Family, villagers, and a centuries-old way of life are all part of his record. The book is organised in accord with his own early exploration of his widening world. He examines his infant sensations, his cottage, his yard, his village and Cotswold valley, then local superstitions, village education, his neighbours, public tragedies, private life-stories, his childhood games, village celebrations, sexual initiations, and the eventual changes as his childhood, his close family life, and the traditional village life pass away for ever.

Detailed summaries

Chapter 1: First Light

The four sections of Lee's first chapter, set in June, summer, autumn, and a cold, blustery November, present the first months of young Laurie's experience in his tiny Cotswold village. Laurie's mother and his sisters, Marjorie, Dorothy, and Phyllis, are introduced. In the first section the eight members of his family move into their stone cottage. Three-year-old Laurie is lost in the tall grass, rescued by his sisters, stuffed with currants, and put on the floor to watch his sisters and his distracted, talkative mother bring flowers and order into the house. In the second section Laurie learns new things—dressing, opening latched doors, whistling—and explores his new environment. In his bedroom, he imagines stories about the knots in the boarded ceiling; in his yard he discovers death in the carcasses of bird, snake, and cat; in the scullery he learns the magical properties of water and enjoys the array of cleaned vegetables about to be made into stew. In the third section Laurie wakens with his eyes gummed shut; opening them with his sisters' help, he sees falling leaves on fire (with colour) and learns about autumn. Going down to the kitchen, they see his mother giving breakfast to a soldier, a deserter who sleeps in the woods and is later caught by the police. Lee here briefly gives his three-year-old's impressions of the First World War. In the fourth section the sisters are left in charge of the family while Mrs Lee goes to visit her soldier husband; in her absence the house is in an uproar and the war ends. They go into the village to watch the celebration: bonfires, people enjoying their drunkenness, dancing, a fight, a chimney fire at the schoolhouse.

NOTES AND GLOSSARY:
In this chapter, Lee gives a three-year-old's perceptions and misconceptions: small in relation to objects around him, Laurie crawls among 'forests' of household objects; he believes autumn is a place and the war's end means the end of the world. Lee uses metaphors and similes (often of water) to communicate the child's sense of adventure.

the Kaiser: Wilhelm (William) II (1859–1941), Emperor of Germany and King of Prussia from 1888 to 1918.

Chapter 2: First Names

Lee's second chapter, divided into three sections, begins in dark winter with peace and the men returning from war; it ends in the 'long hot summer of 1921', when soldiers shot their guns at the clouds to bring rain and young Laurie 'knew our long armistice was over' (p. 37). The chapter is less tightly organized than most, but roughly has to do with night-time feelings: dreams, terrors, superstitions, fears the house would be flooded during midnight downpours. Laurie's half-brother Harold and his brothers Jack and Tony are introduced.

In the first section, while giving a lengthy description of sharing his sleeping mother's warm bed, Lee tells of being tricked by his sisters into sleeping elsewhere, his 'first betrayal'. Next he tells of his early terrors (*a*) at imagined marchers advancing with bread-baskets on their heads, (*b*) of the Old Men, 'obviously gods gone mouldy', and (*c*) of Jones's goat, a large but ordinary animal made extraordinary by the villagers' fear and Lee's poetic description. Lee describes other village terrors: the Death Bird, the Bulls Cross Coach, Miss Barraclough's Goose, Hangman's House, and the talented, English-speaking, death-foretelling Two-Headed Sheep.

In the second section Lee turns from local legends to local living curiosities, some feared and some tolerated: violent Cabbage-Stump Charlie; the deaf-mute Albert-the-Devil; the ragged dandy Percy-from-Painswick; smelly and sorrowful Willy the Fish, three tramps called Harelip Harry, Davis the Drag, and Fisty Fill; the tree-root salesman Tusker Tom; the misanthropic but grotesquely smiling Prospect Smiler; the melancholy and incestuous John-Jack; Emmanuel Twinning who wore a blue blanket, lived with his horse, and was so old that five-year-old Laurie thought he was God.

In the third section drought is followed by torrential rains. In a scene with dialogue, Laurie's mother wails and curses vigorously as she urges her boys to save their cottage from flood by sweeping excess water down a tiny drain.

NOTES AND GLOSSARY:
Just as Lee portrays the perceptions of childhood, he also portrays perceptions—now 'outgrown' by the twentieth-century world—of the 'primitive' village. Thus he records the centuries-old superstitions, local horrors, unthinking cruelties, insularity, and naïve wonderment of the villagers.

gibbet:
an upright post with a projecting arm, used for hanging the bodies of executed criminals as a warning to the general populace

Chapter 3: Village School

Divided into nine sections, Lee's third chapter focuses on Laurie's school experiences from the day he first leaves home for the Infant Room, to the day he leaves Miss Wardley's Big Room for the world. In this chapter Lee briefly expresses his strong opinions about English education: 'So our school work was done—or where would we be today? We would be as we are; watching a loom or driving a tractor, and counting in images of fives and tens' (p. 57). He describes at length two teachers (Crabby B. and Miss Wardley) and two students (conveniently, his brothers Jack and Tony).

The first section serves as introduction to Laurie's expanding world: Lee quickly describes the narrow shape and Ice Age origin of the valley, the number and construction of village buildings, the typical occupations of the villagers; he gives fuller attention to the trees ringing the valley, abundant water, and sunlight on remembered slopes. The second section is devoted to four-year-old Laurie's first day of school, and includes (a) the dialogue of his sisters and a surprised and reluctant Laurie arguing over his going to school, (b) a description in sharp, selected details of the frightened Laurie's view when curious schoolchildren first surround him, and (c) a dialogue of Laurie indignantly telling his sisters that the teacher never gave him his gift, even after telling him to 'sit there for the present'.

In the third section, a scene with dialogue, young Laurie innocently claims that the hair net worn by a new assistant teacher, the 'opulent widow', is a wig; she is indignant. The fourth section mentions three infants—Vera, Jo, and Poppy—and describes Laurie's first lesson: he hits Vera on the head to see the stick bounce, discovers everyone is angry at him, hides but is hauled out of hiding, and learns that 'the summons to the Big Room . . . comes . . . for the crime that one has forgotten' (p. 47).

The fifth section first contrasts brother Jack (a studious 'Infant Freak') with Laurie (an indolent 'natural Infant'), then moves with them to the 'adult and tough' Big Room, ruled by sour Crabby B. Giving a character description of this teacher, Lee shows her in early morning action: whacking students with a ruler after growling the Lord's Prayer. Then he shows the rebellion of big, red-fisted Spadge Hopkins, who refuses to sit down, lifts sputtering Crabby to the top of a cupboard, and strolls out of school, leaving the younger school-children stamping their feet in approval.

The sixth section focuses on the jewellery-jingling Miss Wardley, the new Head Teacher, who calls Laurie 'Fat-and-Lazy' and dislikes his steady sniffing. She quickly approves of industrious, brilliant Jack and insolent, witty Tony; Laurie finally wins her praise by writing essays on otters.

In section seven Lee quickly sums up impressions from years of schooling, listing typical schoolroom smells, subjects studied, methods used (such as memorising and chanting in unison), familiar classroom objects, and names of schoolmates. He describes the sudden freshness and freedom of leaving the classroom: the moment alone outside when *en route* to the outhouse; the release of pent-up energies during playtime. In section eight Lee lists unusual occurrences (beatings, tooth-pullings, visits by the prize-awarding Squire and the head-counting Inspector) and usual excuses (including tasks at home, stolen books, headaches, forged notes, and attendance at the funerals of strangers). He mentions the general acceptance of unusual children like the offspring of incestuous John-Jack, and tells the story of the gipsy Rosso, who was beaten by Miss Wardley for stealing food, and thus won the sympathy of his schoolmates. In the last section Lee points out differences between the first days of school and the last, then shows Miss Wardley wistfully saying farewell to students who will never return.

NOTES AND GLOSSARY:

In his essay 'Writing Autobiography' from *I Can't Stay Long* Lee describes the compression required in this chapter: 'Here five thousand hours had to be reduced to fifteen minutes—in terms of reading time—and those fifteen minutes, without wearying the reader, must seem like five thousand hours.'

grizzling: fretting, worrying, complaining
oakum: loosely twisted jute fibre or hemp, used with tar in caulking boats (to make them watertight)

Chapter 4: The Kitchen

In the five sections of Chapter 4, Lee gives an excellent analysis of family members as seen by the growing boy, Laurie, and then presents his home life—centred on the kitchen—on a typical day.

In the first section he describes the father who brought the family together: Mr Lee, a dandy and a grocer's assistant, rapidly acquired two wives (one died) and twelve children (four died), all of whom he deserted when he joined up as a member of the Army Pay Corps during the First World War. In the second section Lee describes the children that he left (Marjorie, Dorothy, Phyllis, Reggie, Harold, Jack and Tony), as well as their three-storey Cotswold house.

The third section takes the family through a typical morning, from Laurie's waking to his brother Jack's questions, to his mother's haphazard serving of breakfast porridge, to the older children's running off to work and the younger being asked to run errands. Section four shows the younger boys' late-afternoon return home, the lighting of the lamps, the mother frying pancakes, Laurie practising the violin, and half the family gathered around the table. Lee stops his narrative to emphasise the importance to the family of a good fire. The fifth section tells of the older children returning home, recounts the family's drowsy evening conversation in the snug kitchen, and shows Laurie falling off to sleep and being carried to bed.

NOTES AND GLOSSARY:
The frequent symmetry of Lee's structure is apparent in this chapter: the order of morning events is almost exactly reversed in the evening, so that both early and late, for example, Laurie is challenged by Jack. Thus Lee gives his chapters unity and coherence. Once again, notice Lee's use of water imagery when young Laurie falls asleep.

treacle: sugar syrup, molasses
ratted: betrayed, informed upon

Chapter 5: Grannies in the Wainscot

The five sections of Chapter 5 are devoted to two old women and their intimate, antagonistic relationship. The first section explains the living arrangements of 'Er-Down-Under (Granny Wallon) and 'Er-Up-Atop (Granny Trill): the Lee family lives in the down-stroke of their T-shaped cottage and the two grannies live on different floors of the top-stroke. Lee characterises tiny Granny Wallon by lovingly following her through the process of making her famous wines, from gathering the flowers and fruits to delightedly sharing the first bottle of 'last year's cowslip' with the enthusiastic Lee family.

In the second section Lee shows the cud-chewing, early-rising Granny Trill during a visit from the younger brothers: she combs her thin hair, angrily mocks Granny Wallon, delicately winds her hair into a bun, eagerly reads of disasters from the almanac (a publication giving information about stars and weather, organised by the days, weeks and months of a particular year), and tells the story of her youth. In the story, the fifteen-year-old girl watches her father, a woodcutter, pinned to the ground by a fallen tree, take an entire day to die. In the third section Lee describes his early enjoyment of the grannies' inky black clothing, and shows Granny Trill elegantly taking snuff, her 'one horrible vice'.

The fourth section shows the Lee family in relation to Granny Trill: the half-sisters decide to cheer her up with a visit and fashion show. Granny Trill is indignant over their flamingo clothing and throws them out. Section five describes the last years of the grannies, who are so alike but dislike each other, who live so close but arrange never to meet. Finally, Granny Trill breaks her hip, goes to bed, and dies; Granny Wallon goes to the funeral, shrieks disapproval over the age stated on the burial plaque, goes home, and dies soon after.

NOTES AND GLOSSARY:
A variety of visits helps to unify this chapter. Granny Wallon visits the Lee family to gossip and bring new wine; Granny Trill is visited by the Lee family. In contrasting scenes, Granny Trill welcomes the visiting Lee brothers, but throws the visiting Lee sisters out of her house.

wainscot: the panelled portion of an interior wall
chivvying: teasing, baiting, or harassing

Chapter 6: Public Death, Private Murder

In the four sections of Chapter 6, Lee recounts four memorable village·events: the murder of Vincent during a Christmas blizzard; the suicide of Miss Flynn in Jones's Pond; the death of old Mr Davies during a cold January; the sudden mutual feebleness of old Joe and Hannah Brown, their separation by the Visiting Spinsters, and their resulting lonely deaths in separate wings of the Workhouse. The reactions of the villagers to the murder and the suicide reveal much of their essential nature.

In the first section, years after being shipped to the Colonies as a poor boy, Vincent returns to the village as a prosperous New Zealand farmer. Displaying his gold watch, he brags of his wealth in a local pub; he is resented by young villagers, beaten up on his way home, and left to die in a howling snowstorm. The village knows everything and is silent; even ten years later, on her deathbed, an old woman stops mumbling about the watch when a policeman listens.

In the second section Lee carefully unfolds the story of the beautiful, white-faced Miss Flynn, who lived on the opposite side of the valley. First he describes her as seen by the visiting Lee family, then describes the effect of her suicide on others: the milkman, Fred Bates, tells how he found her drowned body; the villagers gossip but do not condemn. Lee then describes the moment of suicide, as imagined by Laurie when staring at the pond. Fred Bates, after seeing another body the next day, is shunned by the superstitious villagers.

In the third section, after a fine extended simile comparing the past of the village to a deep-running cave, Lee briefly describes the cantankerous old Davies couple (who look at each other like card-players) as seen during a Lee family visit; old Mr Davies is ill during a second visit and soon dies.

In the last section of the chapter Lee quickly sketches in the mutual dependence of the Browns, who have lived contentedly in the same snug cottage for fifty years. When they become ill and are separated by the Visiting Spinsters, they die, and shortly thereafter, their cottage falls into ruin.

NOTES AND GLOSSARY:
Lee's narrative skill is particularly apparent in the second section of Chapter 6. He maintains chronology for Laurie's experience (visit, kitchen conversation, overheard gossip, musing at the pond) while deftly giving the essentials of a second person's experience in broken chronology (Miss Flynn's motive, the aftermath, her suicide).

pre-Raphaelite: the Pre-Raphaelites were a brotherhood of artists and poets formed in 1848 principally by Dante Gabriel Rossetti (1828–82), William Holman Hunt (1827–1910), and John Everett Millais (1829–96). They reacted against industrialisation and wished for a return to principles of art held by Italians before the painter Raphael (1483–1520). A frequent model for several in the group was Elizabeth Siddal, a beauty with regular features, large eyes, and a mass of abundant hair

wind-harp: aeolian harp, a box-like stringed instrument tuned to be played by the wind

Visiting Spinsters: ladies authorised to dispense charity

Chapter 7: Mother

The character sketch developed in the eight sections of Chapter 7 takes Annie Light Lee from her birth near Gloucester in the 1880s to her death and burial in the village. Beginning in biographical fashion, Lee gives her parentage (Cotswold farmers and a half-hidden link with the Castle), her early schooling under schoolmaster Mr Jolly, her boring adolescence (caring for her brothers and dreaming at the window), and young womanhood (working as maid in various big houses). Lee describes domestic service in the late nineteenth century: little sleep, much work, being summoned by bells, and five pounds a year for fourteen-hour days; warmth, large plain meals, and lusty living. He shows Mrs Lee years later dreamily remembering elegant dinners while dishing up greens and bacon. He retells two stories showing her naïve astonishment at being noticed: in the first, an Indian prince bows low as she enters a forbidden indoor privy; in the second, an entire regiment snaps to attention when she stands alone in the street.

The second section takes Annie Light through her twenties, years she spent in helping her father at the Plough Inn, and tossing rowdies like Pug Sollars out of the door. She then answered a widower's advertisement for a housekeeper.

The third section is long and complex. In it (a) Lee describes her marriage to the widower with four children, her having children of her own, the desertion, and the differences between her impulsive, jaunty spirit and her husband's frightened orderliness; (b) in dialogue, he records his mother's memories of the three or four years her husband admired her stories, songs, and luxurious hair; (c) he describes his mother's impracticality, panic, and wayward extravagance as she struggled to care for seven children; (d) he recounts her endless but unfounded faith in earning money through entering newspaper competitions and in writing to companies in praise of their products; (e) he describes her gaiety, ready emotions, startled screams, and snatches of quick rhymes; (f) he tells of her lack of punctuality and, in dialogue, shows her searching for items and calling to an impatient but waiting bus-driver; (g) he recalls his mother, unable to stop by herself, bicycling to Stroud and into the arms of a waiting clerk; and (h), in three paragraphs, he sums up his mother as 'a disorganized mass of unreconciled denials', a woman whose initial strength and beauty was worn away, but who remained able to feed her children's 'oafish wits with steady, imperceptible shocks of beauty'.

In the fourth section using dialogue, Lee focuses on his mother as an obsessive collector of fine old china, hindered by her poverty but able to obtain a few cracked pieces. In section five, he describes his mother's extraordinary talent for making flowers grow anywhere, and especially in her jungly kitchen garden. In section six Lee retells her story of the Blacksmith and Toffee-Maker. Both lovelorn, the Toffee-Maker prays in church one day for a man, and is overheard by the Blacksmith, who bellows down in god-like voice, 'Will a blacksmith do?', and is later gratefully accepted.

After a paragraph summarising her many contradictions, in section seven Lee describes his mother dreamily playing the piano, dressed in her finest, and waiting, perhaps, for her husband's return. In the last section of the chapter Lee includes a story of her spending half the night making him a large meal after he came home late during the war. Mostly, however, the section describes his mother having grown into acquiescent, pottering old age—until she hears her long-absent husband has died without ever returning to her, relapses into girlhood, and dies shortly afterwards.

NOTES AND GLOSSARY:
Through his mother's history Lee expands the scope of his book, allowing the reader a glimpse of life in a big house and a view of the harsh, brawling life in a typical small country inn.

Edward II: (1284–1327) King of England from 1307 to 1327, when he was forced to abdicate, imprisoned in Berkeley Castle, and there murdered

Oliver Cromwell: (1599–1658) Lord Protector of England from 1653 to his death

yoo-hoo: greeting meant to attract attention of someone at a distance

Chapter 8: Winter and Summer

In Chapter 8, Lee condenses a childhood of summer and winter days into an account of one typical winter day and one typical summer day. In the first section Laurie wakes to a frozen world on the first day of winter, and goes down to the kitchen to hear the milkman telling of birds freezing in mid-air; he eats, makes handwarmers from old cocoa tins, and goes outside to stand in the cold with friends. They help Farmer Wells to feed his cows, then slide on the newly frozen pond, gather wood, and arrive home late for tea. Shifting to the week before Christmas, Lee describes how after stacking the wood and having tea, Laurie goes out to join the Choir for carolling. The boys choose a leader, stop to sing at the Big House and receive the Squire's tribute, sing at house after house down the valley, fight over Boney's singing flat, and finally arrive at Joseph's farm, where, singing 'As Joseph was a walking' under a cold starry sky, they think of the first Christmas night.

In the second section Laurie wakes on a hot June morning and sees on his ceiling the shadows of swans. Later he helps to groom Brown's horse and watches the Brown family drive off in search of a breeze. In the heat nothing else moves. Finally he joins the crippled Sixpence Robinson and his family in soaking pet pigeons before watching them fly, and in playing a lame-legged game of cricket. In the third section Lee gives a catalogue of summer smells, sights, and sensations, then tells of the gang gathering to play Fox and Hounds during all the warm moonlit night.

NOTES AND GLOSSARY:
Lee has carefully made companion pieces of his two descriptions; for example, each begins with waking, tells about birds, shows Laurie helping an adult with animals, describes Jones's Pond at length, describes the evening activities of the gang, and ends with a lovely evocation of the still valley late at night.

water-butt:	a large cask or barrel containing water
humours:	essential temperaments, dispositions

Chapter 9: Sick Boy

The five sections of Chapter 9 are focused upon young Laurie's childhood illnesses. In the first section Lee mentions that he was christened at birth, but that against expectations, he survived the day, a second formal christening, a host of childhood illnesses, and near burial at the hands of a helpful neighbour, Mrs Moore. The latter episode is cheerfully given in a dialogue between Mrs Lee, in bed after the birth of Tony, and a bored Dorothy. In the second section Lee mentions the death of his much-mourned sister Frances, and portrays at length the fearful fantasies and physical sensations he suffered when feverish. In the third section he describes the worst fever, when he woke to find his weeping family surrounding the bed in a death vigil. In section four, he describes the pleasures of waking after a fever, feeling purged, and indulged by a doting mother. In the last section of the chapter Lee lists at length his minor childhood illnesses, and states that his survival proves his hardiness. He then tells of being concussed after being struck by a bicycle; when he recovered, he became more serious, and his sister was in love with the bicyclist.

NOTES AND GLOSSARY:

The chapter is made unusual by Lee's description of time and objects as perceived when distorted by illness: the walls of the room, for example, begin 'to bulge and ripple and roar, to flap like pastry' (p. 159). Lee is shifting chronology; it is well after the middle of the book, in Chapter 9, that he describes his infancy.

cheeked: behaved saucily or impudently toward
rusks: light biscuits or light bread dough baked twice until crisp
blubbing: blubbering, weeping loudly

Chapter 10: The Uncles

Four of the six sections of Chapter 10 are devoted to character sketches of Lee's four best-known uncles; in the first and last sections, he mentions two more: Uncle George on his father's side and Insurance Fred, one of five Light brothers, on his mother's side. The first section serves as an introduction, particularly to the sons of coachman Grandfather Light. All five brothers fought in the First World War: Lee recalls his confused childhood impressions of these 'khaki ghosts . . . warriors stained with battle'.

In the second section, after a brief account of Uncle Charlie's story-telling abilities, Lee lovingly describes this woodman's forest home. He gives a brief chronological account of his uncle's life as a soldier in the Boer War, as a barman in a Rand diamond camp (he was used as a battering ram and got concussion, then disappeared underground in Johannesburg), and as a local woodsman; then he shows Uncle Charlie at work, tenderly planting new seedlings.

Uncle Tom, portrayed in section three, was notable for his mobile eyebrows and his early success with women. Lee humorously tells of his undoing: huge Effie knocked him off his bicycle to say she wanted him, followed him to his new job as tram-conductor, rode up and down on his tram, got him sacked, watched him run away to a brick-quarry, and married an inspector. Much chastened, he married Minnie and became a coachman-gardener.

The fourth section is devoted to roistering Uncle Ray. Laurie once woke to find him in his bed; Lee focuses on this early visit, describing Ray's tattoos, giving snatches of his teasing conversation with the boys, recalling his energetic ways of returning home after drinking bouts, and recording his pursuit by village women and policemen. Uncle Ray was injured when he returned to the Canadian railway camp; he married Elsie and came back to the Cotswolds.

Lee characterises Uncle Sid in section five. He describes (*a*) his bus-driving (in heroic terms); (*b*) his astonishing prowess on the cricket field during the South African War, giving an 1899 score-card as proof; (*c*) his stopping his bus on a village outing, to climb down, and knock a man unconscious for threatening a woman and child; and (*d*) his reaction (given at length and with dialogue) to being sacked for good by the bus company. In a canny bid for his wife's sympathy, Uncle Sid ineffectively attempted suicide each time he was sacked; Lee shows Aunt Alice's distress as she clutches her two black-clad giggling daughters, the Lee brothers' search through Deadcombe Wood at night, and their discovery of an angry Uncle Sid bobbing at the end of a pair of elastic suspenders, outraged at having waited for hours.

In the last section Lee places his uncles in historical context as 'the horsemen and brawlers of another age'.

NOTES AND GLOSSARY:
Lee states that his uncles were 'the true heroes of my early life', and throughout the chapter he successfully maintains that wondering, boyish perspective. He re-creates his uncles' heroism through skilful use of metaphor and hyperbole; often he summarises in broad strokes, as in this description of Uncle Ray: 'while working in the snow-capped Rockies, he blew himself up with dynamite. He fell ninety feet down the Kicking Horse Pass and into a frozen lake'. Elsie 'travelled four thousand miles to repair him. Having plucked him from the ice and thawed him out, she married him and brought him home' (p. 178).

Caliban:	an allusion to 'a savage and deformed Slave' in Shakespeare's *The Tempest* (1610–11)
charabanc:	an open motor coach for sightseeing
megalith:	a very large stone, especially one forming a prehistoric monument

Chapter 11: Outings and Festivals

The four sections of Chapter 11 present family and village celebrations. The first section describes Peace Day 1919. Marjorie has sewn costumes for herself (as Queen Elizabeth I), as well as for Dorothy (Night), Phyllis (a lady in waiting), Jack (Robin Hood), Tony (a market girl), and Laurie (John Bull in top hat and frock coat), and little Poppy Green (Peace). Laurie pushes Poppy off the mantlepiece to see if she can fly with her cardboard wings. The family joins a long parade of costumed villagers marching through the village to the Big House. The Squire gives Laurie a prize; Lee still has a sepia photograph from that day.

In the second section Lee briefly tells of family outings to gather berries at the far end of the valley, then describes an all-day family outing to Sheepscombe to visit Uncle Charlie, his family, and 'our Gramp'. They leave early, walk over the hills, spend the day, and retrace their steps, with Mrs Lee leading the way and reciting poetry.

The third section focuses on annual Choir Outings, especially one to Weston-super-Mare. When the villagers, travelling in five chara-bancs, finally arrive, the tide is out, but they scatter and enjoy the seaside town. The young boys spend their time and money at a penny arcade on the pier, where Laurie is fascinated by a penny-machine re-enactment of a hanging. The villagers then make their drowsy way home.

The fourth section presents the Parochial Church Tea and Annual Entertainment. Lee describes the home rehearsals, the preparation of the schoolroom, the greetings of the misty-eyed Squire and the irritable vicar, the gorging on ham, buns, cakes and tea, and the clearing away of debris. He moves on to the Entertainment, describing his nervousness before a duet with Eileen Brown, their pleasure when the music is well received, and his enjoyment of the rest of the programme (organist Mr Crosby as comic, the cursing Major Doveton with his banjo, odd ballads by Mrs Pimbury, an odder song by Baroness von Hodenburg).

NOTES AND GLOSSARY:

Queen Elizabeth:	(1533–1603) Queen of England from 1558 to 1603
Robin Hood:	a legendary twelfth-century English outlaw who lived with his followers in Sherwood Forest and robbed the rich to give to the poor
John Bull:	a personification of England and Englishmen
minim:	anything very small
soppy:	sentimental
yokels:	rustics, country persons
toffs:	town dandies

Chapter 12: First Bite at the Apple

The five sections of Chapter 12 are focused on Laurie's first sexual experiences. The first section describes his ritually playing 'doctor', quietly gazing at the cool, milk-green body of shy, silent Jo. The second section contains a brief, important essay on village morality. The village laughed at early sex-games, was tolerant about most things, and punished directly, without reference to law, when it saw fit. Using a map metaphor, in section three Lee talks about the village children as travellers all going in the same direction toward adulthood. In the fourth section Laurie helps with haymaking one hot summer afternoon; although he tells Rosie he is not thirsty, he follows her down the fields and under a wagon to a hidden jug of hard cider, takes a long drink and looks at Rosie again. The afternoon is described as idyllic; that evening Laurie shows off to Rosie on the way home, and sings fierce hymns that night until his brothers march him into the house and to bed. Finally, section five describes the Brith Wood rape, planned, but never performed. In dialogue, Lee recounts how he and five friends plan to rape sixteen-year-old Lizzy Berkeley, who walks about scribbling messages of God's love on beech trees. The next Sunday after church, they wait in the woods and are relieved when she does not come; then she does, and they miserably accost her. She hits them with her bag of crayons and trots off down the hill. Lee ends his account of the coming of age of the village children by referring to their adult lives: Boney marries a farm-widow; Walt goes to sea; Jo marries a baker, Rosie a soldier; and Bet goes to Australia.

NOTES AND GLOSSARY:
Lee constructs his book in accord with Laurie's widening knowledge of his world: *Cider with Rosie* moves effectively from innocence to experience. The chapter's title, 'First Bite at the Apple', is both a cheerful reference to Laurie's first draught of Rosie's hard apple cider and an allusion to Adam's first bite of the apple handed to him by Eve, and his subsequent fall from innocence.

daft: gently crazy, weak-witted, foolish

Chapter 13: Last Days

In the five sections of Chapter 13, Lee focuses on change. The first paragraphs of the first section contain an essay on the tranquillity of life regulated by the seasons and limited by the eight miles an hour of the horse. Stating that the traditional way of life seemed strongest just before it changed, Lee writes about the unquestioned authority of the Church as he knew it. He describes a typical Sunday (learning the Collect at breakfast, rushing off to Sunday School, attending the Morning Service, and later attending Evensong) and describes Harvest Festival, in which the church is decorated with grains and vegetables.

In the second section Lee briefly documents other changes: the death of the Squire and the sale of his estate; the marriage of young couples out of church; the confiscation by an angry vicar of Laurie's copy of *Sons and Lovers*; the death of other old people representative of a time now past. In the third section Lee describes how his close family life changed with the courting of the girls. Lee tells how it all started on the day of the boiler-works fire, describes evenings around the piano with the young men, and re-creates a hot day's picnic led by gallant Mrs Lee. In section four he describes a family argument, and eventual peace-making, over a young man's desire to marry one of the girls. In the final section Lee sums up the changes in his family and village, and briefly alludes to the changes in himself, now nearly grown-up, lonely, and beginning to write poetry.

NOTES AND GLOSSARY:
Note that one by one Lee says good-bye to the things he has emphasised in the book. His emphasis on 'last' in this chapter balances his emphasis on 'first' in the opening chapters, and rounds off the book.

apologist: a person who, in speaking or writing, justifies or defends a faith or doctrine

the Collect: a short prayer suited to the occasion or season

Part 3

Commentary

The nature and purpose of the work

Laurie Lee's *Cider with Rosie* is autobiography: its central character, narrator, and author discernibly the same.

The purpose of autobiography has always been to reveal and comment upon the life of the person who himself is writing the work. Thus in the fourth century, in what is often considered the first autobiography, St Augustine (354–430) presented his life before and after conversion to Christianity, writing his *Confessions* as a lesson for others, and judging his early life harshly. Benvenuto Cellini, writing between 1557 and 1562 what is now considered as one of the most vital documents produced in the Italian Renaissance, used his *Autobiography* to express his own immense pride in his life in Florence, Rome, and Paris as the most renowned metalsmith of his age; he wrote with equal vigour of love, murder, and art. In a famous autobiography of the eighteenth century, the wise and practical American inventor and statesman Benjamin Franklin (1706–90) attributed his early success to industry and thrift. Also in the eighteenth century, in his *Confessions* begun in 1765, the French author Jean Jacques Rousseau (1712–78) described not only the facts of his life but his own deepest feelings in an intensely personal autobiography still acclaimed for its candour. These four men wrote four of the most notable early autobiographies. The *genre* increased in popularity in the nineteenth century, and in the twentieth century, of course, personal 'confessions' abound.

Unlike those of some of his more famous predecessors, Laurie Lee's aims as an autobiographer are modest. As he has recorded in his essay 'Writing Autobiography' in *I Can't Stay Long*, he believes 'an ego that takes up too much of a book can often wither the rest of it. . . . The autobiographer's self can be a transmitter of life that is larger than his own—though it is best that he should be shown taking part in that life and involved in its dirt and splendours.' Thus in *Cider with Rosie*, Lee's concern is less often that of showing what was specifically individual about his own life—a preoccupation of autobiographers since Cellini—than of showing his part in a communal way of life shared by villagers in the Cotswolds for almost a thousand years, but now lost: as he puts it in 'Writing Autobiography',

'The end of my childhood also coincided by chance with the end of a rural tradition—a semi-feudal way of life which had endured for nine centuries, until war and the motor-car put an end to it.' Clarifying his intentions in writing *Cider with Rosie*, he affirms, 'I was less interested . . . in giving a portrait of myself than in recording the details of that small local world . . . It seemed to me that my own story would keep, whereas the story of the village would not, for its words, even as I listened, were being sung for the last time and were passing into perpetual silence.' Lee's first autobiographical volume is thus thronged with villagers: about 145 people are presented on its pages. He recounts village stories of the lives of others, in addition to recording his own early life and the lives of all his family. He includes school-mates and teachers, friends and neighbours in his accounts of village life winter and summer, weekdays and holidays. A main motive in writing *Cider with Rosie*, Lee states in 'Writing Auto-biography', was 'celebration: to praise the life I'd had and so preserve it'.

A record of Lee as child and adolescent

Lee's portrait of himself is among the least clearly defined in the gallery of characters found in *Cider with Rosie*. Very often he is merely a recording consciousness. After the first chapters, he has suggested, he deliberately made himself 'less a character than a presence, a listening shadow, a moving finger, recording the flavours of the days, the ghosts of neighbours, the bits of winter, gossip, death' ('Writing Autobiography').

Moreover, when the young Lee does appear, the author usually makes him representative of boys growing up in the Cotswolds before everything changed. Thus he is typical in his widening explorations of houses and garden, village and valley. His doing chores at home, his playing evening games like Fox and Hounds, his experiences in the village school, his membership in the church choir, his presence on village outings—all these aspects of his life are presented as perfectly ordinary.

Lee writes 'we' as often as 'I'. He identifies his young self with groups: he is one of the young trio of Lee boys; he is part of the large extended Lee family; he is a member of a small village gang of boys and one of a generation of village young people; he is an unquestioning inhabitant of the village itself. Even at the end of the book, when recounting something as personal as the first sexual encounters of his boyhood, Lee merges his private feelings with those of the group: 'Very soon I caught up with other travellers, all going in the same direction. They received me naturally, the boys and girls

Winston.

of my age, and together we entered the tricky wood' (p. 206).

Even on the few occasions Lee does individualise himself, he never presents his own actions as exceptional or particularly laudable. As a young child he was stubborn, balking angrily when told he was now old enough to sleep without mother or to attend the village school. He was curious. As a matter of course he was devoted to his mother, cherished his half-sisters, and shared a close rivalry with his two true brothers. Lee suggests he was indolent, first a 'natural Infant, content . . . to slop around and whine and idle', and later characterised as 'Fat-and-Lazy' (pp. 48, 52). Occasionally, with his brother Jack, he was enterprising, earning free tickets to the Parochial Church Tea and Annual Entertainment. He was also bright, winning prizes at school, although the author states, 'that's nothing to boast about'. In all his active young life, Laurie was unique only, perhaps, when playing his violin—and then not when he was merely part of the village's Annual Entertainment, but rather when he entertained his mother in the kitchen while she made supper: 'Now and then I got a note just right, and then Mother would throw me a glance . . . old and tired though she was, her eyes were a girl's and it was for looks such as these that I played' (p. 71).

Growing up in his village, Laurie was different not when he was active but when he was ill; a sickly child, he suffered a battery of childhood illnesses. Expectations that he could never survive led to the distinction of being baptised twice, laid out for burial at eighteen months, and 'prayed for in church, just before the collections, twice, on successive Sundays' (p. 164). One of his first memories is of the 'marching of monsters . . . advancing up the valley with their heads stuck in breadbaskets, . . . a result of early headaches' (p. 28). In 'Sick Boy', the one chapter devoted almost solely to himself, Lee records sick nightmares of smiles hung in space, 'smiles without pity, smiles without love . . . expanding in brilliant silence' (p. 159).

If anything besides illness distinguished young Laurie Lee, it was not his deeds, but rather these nightmares when fevered, his dreams during the night, his fantasies when day-dreaming. In these, at least, he felt himself to be unique and even noble. Thus Lee presents his feelings at three when he slept beside his mother: 'It was for me alone that the night came down, for me the prince of her darkness' (p. 27). A moment alone outside the busy schoolroom found him day-dreaming: 'I know I'm something special, a young king perhaps placed secretly here in order to mix with the commoners' (p. 54). When ill, he often almost wept, feverishly thinking about his 'anxious people, the invisible multitudes up and down the land joined in grief at this threat to their King' (p. 158). In these moments of self-exultation, young Laurie was, of course, still typical. The author's gentle self-mockery comes to a close at the end of the book when he shows the newly-adolescent Laurie being just like all the others in separating himself from the group: 'I groaned from solitude, blushed when I stumbled, . . . made long trips through the rain on my bicycle, stared wretchedly through lighted windows, grinned wryly to think how little I was known, and lived in a state of raging excitement' (p. 231).

A record of Lee's family

His mother

Lee devotes a chapter to his mother's life, from her birth in the early 1880s to her death some sixty-five years later. In addition, he makes her presence felt throughout the book. For example, after Lee's long description of his bouts of fever in 'Sick Boy', his mother suddenly re-enters the chapter, 'carolling upstairs with . . . breakfast, bright as a wind-blown lark' (p. 166).

Lee does not stress his mother's unfailing compassion, but rather shows it in several small scenes. A deserter asking for tea on her doorstep is taken inside and given a large breakfast, and although her five brothers were in the armed services, Mrs Lee 'sighed and was sad over the poor man' when he was finally caught (p. 20). Mrs Lee takes time to visit neighbours who are ill, weary, or old, and she makes excuses for their weaknesses. 'There are others more wicked, poor soul', she tells her boys when they question her about Miss Flynn, and when that unhappy woman confesses she cannot sleep for having been so bad, Mrs Lee makes 'a clucking sympathetic sound', and claims the west wind is 'bad for the nerves' (p. 100). Visiting the old Davies couple regularly, Mrs Lee knows when to offer help: 'Let me finish the gruel . . . You're trying to do too much', she tells the old woman who is bewildered by her husband's final illness. She scolds her boys for imitating old Granny Trill: 'Don't mock . . . The poor, poor soul— alone by herself all day. . . . You girls ought to pop up and pay her a visit' (p. 89). Mrs Lee's compassion extends to other creatures as well. 'It's wicked', she says at the first cold blast of winter. 'The poor, poor birds' (p. 136).

Always, Mrs Lee places others before herself. Thus, among other things, she has raised three families: a bright, imaginative student, she unquestioningly left school at thirteen to replace her ill mother in raising the five young boys of the family. Going into domestic service at seventeen as scullery-maid, housemaid, nursemaid, and eventually parlour-maid, she left that work when her mother died and her father needed her help at his small inn. At thirty, she took a job as housekeeper for a widower with four children, married him, had four children, and was deserted by him. Without complaint, Mrs Lee raised 'both his families, which she did out of love and pity, out of unreasoning loyalty and a fixed belief that he would one day return to her . . .' (p. 61).

Lee shows his mother to have been endlessly hard-working, most often in the kitchen. Once, during the Second World War and after old Mrs Lee had lost all sense of time, Laurie came home late at night and was wakened near dawn by his mother with a great platter of food: 'The boy had come home and he had to have supper, and she had spent half the night preparing it' (p. 134). During earlier years of full command, she kept so busy around the stove she never had time to sit down to a meal: 'Eating with one hand, she threw on wood with the other, raked the ashes, and heated the oven, put on a kettle, stirred the pot, and spread out some more shirts on the guard' (p. 72). Her one voiced complaint in the book occurs when rising water has flooded into her kitchen: 'I can't *think* what I've done to be so troubled and tried. And just when I got the house straight. . . . Look out with that damn-and-cuss bucket!' (p. 39).

Certainly Mrs Lee, disorganised and erratic, created some difficulties for herself. She was never on time, much to the acute embarrassment of her boys. She was forever looking for items she had mislaid: shoes, gloves, matches, corsets. She had troubles managing her household: 'There would be no meat at all from Monday to Saturday, then on Sunday a fabulous goose; no coal or new clothes for the whole of the winter, then she'd take us all to the theatre' (p. 122). Her emotions were as erratic as her housekeeping and were expressed as freely as those of a child. Lee writes with ironic sentiment: 'I can still seem to hear her blundering about the kitchen: shrieks and howls of alarm, an occasional oath, a gasp of wonder, a sharp command to things to stay still' (p. 123).

When she could steal moments away from her work, however, Lee's mother revealed herself to be a quiet, pensive person. As an adolescent, in moments away from her rough-and-tumble brothers, she 'would put up her hair, squeeze her body into a tight-boned dress, and either sit by the window, or walk in the fields—getting poetry by heart, or sketching the landscape in a delicate snowflake scribble' (p. 114). In her lonely twenties, when she was not needed to handle the drunks at her father's inn, she 'would dress in her best and sit out on the terrace, reading, or copying flowers' (p. 120). In her later life, when all the children were in bed, she 'would change into her silk, put on her bits of jewellery, and sit down to play the piano' (p. 133); her music on such evenings expressed all her loneliness and her faithful love for the man who had abandoned her.

The hardships of her life are not stressed by Lee, perhaps because his mother most often ignored them herself. Her education sacrificed to her brothers' care when she was growing up, her young womanhood wasted in a brawling inn, her marriage broken by a prim, irresponsible husband, her only daughter dead at the age of four, her days filled with the care of seven children, poor and overworked, nonetheless, Mrs Lee 'possessed an indestructible gaiety which welled up like a thermal spring' (p. 123). She had a gift for growing things, and filled her house and her garden with flowers. She sang hymns on walks with her children, played the piano, and encouraged her young son's practising the violin. She quoted poetry at length and often created rhymes in sharp, quick snatches. She told stories well: Lee gives in her own words the story of the Indian prince at the privy and a second story of a regiment parading before her with 'Eyes right!'. She was in awe of the privileged life she had glimpsed while a servant in great houses: she cherished fine china and bought what cracked pieces she could afford; she knew the 'family trees of all the Royal Houses of Europe' (p. 126). On village outings, she 'pointed out landmarks and lectured the sleepers on points of historical interest' (pp. 193–4); she planned elaborate picnics for bored future sons-in-law and, undaunted, 'knew soon enough when people turned sour and moved mountains to charm them out of it' (p. 227). Exuberantly walking with her children to the next valley, she stopped often to admire the view: 'What a picture . . . Green as green' (p. 188). Thus she taught her children to appreciate the beauty of nature and of art, and even now, Lee reports, his 'pleasure pays some brief duty to her' (p. 127).

His sisters

Lee's three older half-sisters, Marjorie, Dorothy, and Phyllis, play a significant role in *Cider with Rosie*. Described only briefly in 'Sick Boy' is his much-mourned sister Frances, a dark frail child who was his mother's only daughter, who watched quietly by his crib during his entire sickly first year, and who died quietly when she was four.

The reader's first glimpse of the three half-sisters is through Laurie's three-year-old eyes: 'Faces of rose, familiar, living; huge shining faces hung up like shields between me and the sky' (p. 9). Frequently, throughout the book—as in his description of his first morning of school—Lee does not distinguish between the three: 'my sisters surrounded me, wrapped me in scarves, tied up my bootlaces, thrust a cap on my head, and stuffed a baked potato in my pocket' (p. 43). Together, then, they comfort him during his nightmares, cajole and flatter him into sleeping alone, and threaten him into docility: 'Boys who don't go to school get put into boxes, and turn into rabbits, and get chopped up Sundays' (p. 43). During the first two chapters, however, the two oldest girls develop distinct voices, and in 'The Kitchen', Lee spends considerable time establishing each girl's separate identity.

Marjorie is the oldest, responsible enough at fourteen to be left alone as head of the household, although not yet capable of running it smoothly. When Dorothy urges excitement, Marjorie's typical response is 'You know we can't leave the kids' (p. 21). Marjorie is even-tempered and 'dreamily gentle'; she is tall, green-eyed and blonde. Lee describes her as 'wearing her beauty like a kind of sleep' (p. 61). Marjorie eventually works at a milliners' store in Stroud and is seen trimming a new hat in 'The Kitchen'. Moreover, Marjorie is a skilled seamstress. She it is who sewed the Peace Day costumes described in 'Outings and Festivals': 'No makeshift, rag-bag cobbling either; Marjorie had worked as though for a wedding' (p. 184). And she it is who pieces together the flapper finery the three sisters display before Granny Trill's outraged eyes in 'Grannies in the Wainscot'.

Dorothy, much more volatile than her older sister, is always ready for excitement or a good story. Lee's metaphor for Marjorie is a 'steady flame'; for Dorothy it is 'spark and tinder' and 'a firework'. Dorothy is 'junior clerk in a decayed cloth-mill by a stream', but work at this cloth-mill was dull drudgery. Lee describes her as 'an active forager who lived on thrills, provoked adventure, and brought home gossip'. Occasionally she sat quietly, and then, Lee says, she became 'a fairy-tale girl, blue as a plum, tender, and sentimental' (p. 62).

Phyllis, three years younger than Marjorie and about ten years older than Laurie, is described as 'a tobacco-haired, fragile girl, who carried her good looks with an air of apology, being the junior and somewhat shadowed' (p. 62). She is seen in the first two chapters as weeping over the vegetables when Marjorie takes charge, and as having hysterics in the pantry over the appearance of Jones's goat. In 'The Kitchen', Lee describes her as gravely and tunelessly singing the boys to sleep, and later as polishing the silver while Dorothy writes a love-letter. She works at Boots-and-Shoes.

His brothers and brothers-in-law

Young Lee had two older half-brothers called Reggie and Harold, two true brothers called Jack and Tony from his father's second family, and eventually three brothers-in-law called Maurice, Leslie and Harold.

His half-brother Reggie is mentioned only once, as he grew up in the household of his father's mother. His half-brother Harold makes brief appearances in *Cider with Rosie*: he shares a bedroom with Laurie and Jack, cleans his bicycle in 'The Kitchen', leaves at six 'with an angry shout for the lathe-work he really loved' (p. 68), frog-marches Laurie to bed after the bout with Rosie's cider, and both mends the chairs and re-upholsters the furniture before finally bringing home his girl. 'Handsome, bony, and secretive', he loves his absent father and is 'unhappy more often than not' (p. 63). Young Laurie knows he might die when, among the anxious people around his sickbed, 'even Harold, who could usually shrug off emotion', looks 'pale and strained in the candlelight' (p. 163).

The three brothers-in-law, all very much in love, are present only in the last chapter, 'Last Days'. Maurice, Marjorie's fiancé, is described as 'handsome, curly-haired, a builder of barges, very strong, and entirely acceptable'. Dorothy's shy Leslie, a local scout-master, is 'tactful and diffident, giving short sharp laughs' (p. 225) at Mrs Lee's jokes. Harold the Bootmaker, whom Phyllis is to marry, charms the family with his Latin good looks, piano-playing, and songs about old-fashioned mothers.

The three 'true brothers' are at times described as a trio. They are together in the Big Room, play Fox and Hounds during the long summer evenings, and go carolling with other boys from the Choir on a cold night before Christmas. It is the slightly older Jack, however, who is singled out as Lee's close companion: 'We played together, fought and ratted, built a private structure around us, shared the same bed till I finally left home, and lived off each other's brains' (p. 63).

Jack, as he advances in the course of the book from Infant Room to Big Room to Grammar School, is at times set apart by his intelligence. He bullies his teachers in a 'cold clear voice' and makes other students uncomfortable. An 'Infant Freak' in the village school, he sits 'pale in his pinafore, gravely studying, commanding the teacher to bring him fresh books, or to sharpen his pencils, or to make less noise' (p. 47). An 'accepted genius' in the Big Room, Jack is 'absolved . . . from mortal contacts', and is described as thus 'left in a corner where his flashes of brilliance kept him twinkling away like a pin-table' (pp. 52–3). Even when portrayed in the midst of the family, in the middle of the noisy kitchen, Jack sits working on his 'inscrutable homework' (p. 71). A mixture of pride, humour, and chagrin can be detected in Lee's descriptions of his brother Jack; love and rivalry were equally strong. The full day described in 'The Kitchen' begins and ends with Jack's abrupt challenges as Laurie gets out of a warm bed and returns to a cold one: 'What's the name of the king, then?' 'Say, think of a number! . . . Double it' (pp. 65, 77). Jack avoids running errands when it is his turn; known as The Slider, he works out a method of gaining more than his share of food from his mother's erratic serving spoon. Lee admits ruefully, 'Many the race I've lost to him thus, being just that second slower' (p. 69).

Lee's own younger brother, Tony, the baby of the family, the odd one out among the seven children, is described as a 'brooding, imaginative solitary' (p. 63). Not having reached adolescence even by the end of *Cider with Rosie*, Tony is always portrayed as very young: he asks aloud for drums in church during Harvest Festival; he talks to the cat (p. 72) and croons a 'cotton reel story' to himself as he plays in 'The Kitchen' after tea (p. 74). Lee sums up Tony at school in a sentence: 'He would sit all day picking holes in blotting paper, his large eyes deep and knowing, his quick tongue scandalous, his wit defiant, his will set against all instruction' (p. 53).

His uncles, aunts, and cousins

Lee considered his family to have been 'especially well-endowed with uncles' (p. 169), and he devotes a chapter, 'The Uncles', to them and their families. The six uncles are not all treated at the same length; Uncle George, for example, on Lee's father's side, is described briefly as a 'thin, whiskered rogue, who sold newspapers in the streets, lived for the most part in rags, and was said to have a fortune in gold' (p. 169). Lee's mother's brothers—Uncles Charlie, Tom, Ray, Sid, and Fred—are mentioned as 'huge remote men' in 'First Light' and mythologised as cavalry men in the First World War at the start of 'The Uncles': 'a fist of uncles aimed at the foe, riders of hell and apocalypse, each one half-man, half-horse' (p. 169). Then, four of the uncles are discussed in turn in considerable detail; the fifth, Insurance Fred, was lost to the family 'through prosperity and distance' (p. 183).

Uncle Charlie, a forester, lived with Aunt Fanny and their four children in the woods, in a cottage typically 'wrapped in aromatic smoke, with winter logs piled in the yard, while from eaves and doorposts hung stoats'-tails, fox-skins, crow-bones, gin-traps, and mice' (pp. 170–1). Uncle Tom, a quietly spoken coachman-gardener, and his tiny wife Minnie are similarly characterised by their surroundings: 'Life in their small, neat stable-yard . . . seemed . . . more toylike than human' (p. 172).

Eventually married to Aunt Elsie, in his early days daring Uncle Ray built railroads in Canada and was a 'prospector, dynamiter, buffalo-fighter' (p. 174). Focusing at length on one early visit, Lee shows this uncle to have been a lusty, brawling, drinking man, with 'leather-beaten face', 'far-seeing ice-blue eyes', and wondrous tattoos. Uncle Ray, affirms Lee, was 'the hero of our school-boasting days' (p. 174).

Eventually married to Aunt Alice and father of two daughters,

Uncle Sid first fought in both the Boer War and the First World War, played cricket for the Army with astounding skill, and heroically drove a double-decker bus: 'Runaway roarer, freighted with human souls, stampeder of policemen and horses—it was Uncle Sid with his mighty hands who mastered its mad career' (p. 178). Moody and majestic, this uncle is faintly diminished in stature later in life when, beset by alcohol and rheumatism, and often fired, he stages false suicides to escape scoldings.

His father

Lee's father married twice and had twelve children, of whom eight survived. His first wife died; he left his second. He put his oldest son into the care of his mother and left the seven children remaining from two marriages with his second wife. He sent her money regularly but it was never enough. The reader sees this father as his children saw him, in portraits hung in many rooms and in the memories of a wife who waited thirty years for his return. Early portraits display 'a handsome though threadbare lad, tall and slender, and much addicted to gloves, high-collars, and courtly poses' (p. 60). In a later portrait, off to what Lee calls his 'clerk-stool war' (p. 61), he is dressed in khaki like all the others, although young Lee confuses him with the Kaiser: 'His picture hung over the piano, trim, haughty, with a badged cap and a spiked moustache' (p. 24). Particularly remote from early morning confusion in 'The Kitchen', 'Father in his pince-nez up on the wall looked down like a scandalized god' (p. 67).

In *Cider with Rosie* Lee twice gives his father slightly more attention. At the start of 'The Kitchen', he summarises his father's early history as 'a grocer's assistant, a local church organist, an expert photographer, and a dandy' (p. 60). Lee's irony becomes marked when he describes the First World War as his Father's great opportunity to desert his family and become a Civil Servant. Later, in 'Mother', Lee allots several paragraphs to the man who overwhelmed her, this 'rather priggish young man, with his devout gentility, his airs and manners, his music and ambitions, his charm, bright talk, and undeniable good looks' (p. 121). In quick snatches of remembered conversation, Lee gives the three or four years of laughter, admiration, and music upon which Mrs Lee 'fed . . . for the rest of her life'. In spite of her life-long love, the two were clearly mismatched: Lee's father was a 'frightened man', who longed for the safety of 'the protective order of an unimpeachable suburbia' (p. 121), obtained it, and died a fitting death, 'cranking his car in a Morden suburb' (p. 135).

A record of the villagers

Eccentrics and outcasts

Lee constructs *Cider with Rosie* in rough accord with his own childhood explorations. Among the 'First Names' he records outside his own household are those of local eccentrics easily distinguished from the general lot of villagers. Thus the second chapter includes thumbnail sketches of the following: the quarrelsome pigman, Cabbage-Stump Charlie; a deaf-mute beggar, Albert the Devil; a half-witted, ragged dandy called Percy-from-Painswick; sad, scratching and smelly Willy the Fish; tree-root salesman Tusker Tom; three circuit tramps called Harelip Harry, Davis the Drag, and Fisty Fill; the misanthropic Prospect Smiler; gloomy John-Jack, who lived above the valley with his sister Nancy and their five children; and old Emmanuel Twinning, who dressed in sky-blue blankets and cosily shared his house with his old grey horse. Later in his childhood young Laurie became aware of other misfits, and their stories are related in later chapters. In the 'Village School', he encountered Rosso, the dark gipsy boy who was accepted by the schoolboys only after a caning by the teacher. He learned hushed details about Vincent, a local-boy-made-good by cattle-farming in the Colonies and murdered for his boasting when he returned home. Treated more tolerantly by the villagers was the beautiful, solitary, haunted Miss Flynn, who nonetheless drowned herself in Jones's pond. An outcast was created by her death, however, for Fred Bates, the scrawny milkboy who not only found her body but saw a man crushed to death in Stroud the next day, was avoided for years. Lee carefully portrays these last three unfortunates in 'Public Death, Private Murder'.

Village boys and girls

As recounted in 'Village School', Laurie first confronted the village children when he was four; the roll called in that chapter and elsewhere includes at least eleven girls and eleven boys. In the following chapters, these friends are briefly glimpsed at various stages in their childhood and adolescence; through scattered phrases, Lee economically shows an entire generation of young villagers growing up. Thus, for example, blonde Jo clings to her best girlfriend in the Infant Room, later gravely undresses and allows the adolescent Laurie to touch her, and is said eventually to have married a baker and grown fat. In 'Village School', the boys smirk at Betty Gleed; eleven and brazen in 'First Bite at the Apple', she still attracts them, but leaves as an adult to live in Australia.

In addition to Jo and Betty, the girls of the village include Poppy
Green, Sis and Sloppy Robinson, Edna from Bull's Cross, Carrie and
Rosie Burdock, Vera, Eileen Brown, and Lizzy Berkeley. In 'Village
School', Laurie hits Vera on her springy hair; in 'Outings and
Festivals' he pushes Poppy, Jo's chum, into the fireplace. He plays a
grown-up duet with Eileen. He kisses Rosie and drinks her cider in
'First Bite at the Apple', and plans to rape Lizzy. Rosie is sly,
provocative, and superbly self-assured; stubby, blue-eyed Lizzy is
naïve, odd enough to chalk biblical texts on beech trees, but happily
sufficiently quick on her feet.

Among the boys, most frequently seen is the bully, Walt Kerry,
who demands tribute from Laurie (and his answers to homework
questions as well) in 'Village School' and enjoys power (the eked-out
information about ice) in 'Winter and Summer'. Often excluded, Walt
makes a bossy member of the gang when the boys play Fox and
Hounds, go Christmas carolling, and plan rape. Walt, however, sits
quietly when teachers call him 'a great hulking lout of an oaf' (p. 56);
it takes the older, tougher Spadge Hopkins to defy the teacher
Crabby B. successfully (pp. 50–2). On the other end of the scale is
meek, adoring, little Jim Fern.

Among Laurie's closer friends are Horace and Boney Harris, both
eager to fight even at Christmas (pp. 146–7). Fat-faced, shifty Bill
Shepherd, who always looks caught-in-the-act, is mentioned chiefly
for thinking up the Brith Wood rape; Clergy Green, a 'preaching
maniac' mentioned much more often, reacts to the plans with his
'whinnying, nervous giggle' (p. 212). Sixpence the Tanner, cheerful
though crippled, is also included in the scheme; during earlier summer
afternoons, he dunked pigeons and played cricket with his brother
Sammy and Stosher Robinson.

Frequently, Lee portrays the members of his gang in general terms;
in 'Winter and Summer', for example, he distinguished merely
between the blue, shivering 'thin ones' and the 'fat ones', all 'rosy and
blowing like whales' (p. 138). But even when he mentions their
names, Lee presents his friends as typical and their actions as
habitual. Thus one game of Fox and Hounds stands for all the summer
evening games of Lee's own childhood, and for those of countless
Cotswold generations as well.

Teachers at the village school

In 'Village School', Lee mentions a series of teachers: in the Infant
Room were a beautiful sixteen-year-old junior teacher, a comforting
young teacher in braids, and eventually a tall opulent widow, who
doused herself with lavender water and wore a hairnet which young

Laurie rudely called a wig; in the Big Room were Crabby B. and later Miss Wardley of the jingling glass jewellery. As he did in childhood, the adult Lee spends more time on these latter two, recreating Crabby B.'s mode of speech ('I will not have it. I'll not, I say') and that of Miss Wardley ('How about bringing a hanky tomorrow? I'm sure we'd all be grateful'). He compares Crabby to a turkey-gobbler and a yellow cat (she had the skin and voice of the first, the colouring and sudden motion of the second), focuses on her rigid discipline rather than her lackadaisical lessons, and writes a scene showing her ineptitude when defied by the red-fisted fourteen-year-old farm-boy, Spadge Hopkins. Replacing Crabby, Miss Wardley used a 'looser but stronger' rein; sharp-tongued, but patient enough, she cared most for birds and flowers, drawing and singing, and wistfully wished her students good luck when they grew up and left school.

Young men and women of the village

Lee's remembered valley is alive with villagers at work. Among these are his five teachers, whom he shows in the classroom and describes in some detail, but there are many others busy in the shops, at the forge, and on the farms. Mr Vick, the shopkeeper, carries his two shopkeys in a basket even during 'Outings and Festivals' (his wife is seen in 'Village School', scolding the gipsy Rosso for stealing food). Lew Ayres still takes up to six passengers in his wagonette on a regular run to Stroud in 'Last Days'; his wife has leisure to gossip at Jones's Pond in 'Public Death, Private Murder'. Willing to take a moment to argue on the job are Dr Wills, who 'don't believe in cutting', and Dr Packer, 'a rigid one for the knife'; Dr Green, appearing in a pair of corduroy bloomers, seems less professional than they are. Although his own son is dying and can only look out of the window, Farmer Wells kindly allows the boys to be around his barn; he works the farm on the edge of the village, Joseph the Farmer works at the furthest reach of the valley, and Farmer Lusty apparently does not work, for his oats are rotting in the fields.

The village post-mistress is Mrs Okey; the postman, although he religiously attends Evensong in 'Last Days', less reliably throws his mailbag aside to take a day off in 'Outings and Festivals'. To enjoy the outing, Herbert, the church gravedigger, takes his spade to the beach. Others associated with church work are Mr Crosby, the organist—and amateur comic—and Rex Brown, the organ blower; the latter often irreverently pantomimes the church service and carves girls' names in the church woodwork. Miss Bagnall not only teaches in Sunday School and attends every Evensong, but holds penny dances at which she plays the piano only while the boys and girls behave.

Other women are the Widow White and Widow Pimbury. Miss Birt hangs out her washing in 'Village School', and Miss Cohen, a sour spinster who is perhaps deservedly knocked down by Jones's goat in 'First Names', most remarkably asks about Laurie when he is deathly ill in 'Sick Boy'. No longer working are Major Carvosso and Major Doveton, although the latter retains some skill in playing the banjo and great skill in cursing in both English and Urdu.

By giving his villagers specific names and including exact though brief details, Lee adds to the rich texture of his book, making the reader feel that these are real people, all in their accustomed places, with stories of their own, had he—or they—time to tell them.

Old men and women of the village

Part of Lee's purpose is to record a way of life and its passing, and he pays particular attention to those villagers who most embody it: the old people. Even when very young, Laurie Lee was fascinated by the old villagers he saw around him: he recounts in the fifth chapter his childhood fantasy of commanding a parade of grandmas, 'rank upon rank of hobbling boots, nodding bonnets, flying shawls, and furious chewing faces' (p. 88). Thus he remembers in 'Last Days' old Lottie Escourt, 'peasant shoot of a Norman lord', and Kicker Harris, the 'old coachman, with his top-hat and leggings'. He remembers Mrs Clissold, who sent him on errands and rewarded him with a sleepy nod: 'Mrs Crissole'll recollect 'ee' (p. 224). In 'Public Death, Private Murder' even the old woman, briefly mentioned, who dies steadfastly keeping the secret that her sons possess the murdered Vincent's gold watch is portrayed with sympathy and pride, and Lee devotes half that chapter to the tough old Davies couple and contented Joseph and Hannah Brown. In 'Grannies in the Wainscot', he draws at great length and with love the portraits of Granny Wallon and Granny Trill, two ancients who contrive with steadfast enmity never to see each other. Totally preoccupied by their disdainful rivalry, they in truth live for each other, and Granny Wallon dies shortly after Granny Trill.

The Squire and the vicar

In the years recounted in *Cider with Rosie*, the Squire and the vicar still maintained their traditional, even ceremonial, roles in the village. Thus when as a girl Granny Trill hid in the woods after her father had died, it was the Squire who took responsibility for having her hunted down, washed, set to work and married to a man her father's age. The Squire, by sending her porridge, still kept her alive in her nineties. It was the Squire, in 'Village School', who would pay 'a visit, hand out prizes, and make a misty-eyed speech' (p. 56). On Peace Day in 'Outings and Festivals', he and his ancient mother gave a party for the villagers; much moved by the sight of the village procession winding down his drive, the 'wet-eyed Squire' again gave out prizes. Dressed in a cloak and deer-stalking hat, the Squire yearly started the festivities at the Parochial Church Tea and Annual Entertainment; Lee shows his speech to have been endearingly befuddled: 'When I see you all gathered together here—once more—when I see—when I think. . . . And here you all are!' (p. 198).

As the voice of the Church and the representative of God, the vicar also had great authority in the village; he thunders from his pulpit and confiscates Laurie Lee's copy of *Sons and Lovers* in 'Last Days'. He wears pyjamas under his raincoat when he officiates at the early morning start of the Annual Choir Outing, the better to hurry back to bed (p. 191). Also in 'Outings and Festivals', he is shown in a testy spirit when his audience already knows his joke; he recovers quickly enough and launches into prayer. White-haired and faintly beaming, the vicar is old, as is the Squire; Lee records the passing of their days of greatest influence, when 'the year revolved around the village, the festivals round the year, the church round the festivals, the Squire round the church, and the village round the Squire' (p. 184).

A record of a way of life

The physical appearance of the cottage, village, and valley

Built of stone in the seventeenth century, the Lee family's rented house served first as a small country manor and then as a public beer-house before being divided into 'three poor cottages in one'. Three-storied and shaped as a T, it was occupied by Granny Wallon and Granny Trill in the cross-bar, one on top of the other, and by the eight members of the Lee family in the down stroke. The interior of the house had been 'patched and parcelled' (p. 64), so that rooms entered awkwardly into each other, and 'its attics and passages were full of walled-up doors' (p. 78). The long white attic of the third floor served the half-sisters as a thin-roofed bedroom; Lee's mother and the boys had bedrooms on the second floor. Below this were the scullery and kitchen, the first described in 'First Light', the second, as the most important room in the house, described at length in 'The Kitchen'. Mrs Lee filled the kitchen with a profusion of gathered flowers and weeds; outside its windows, her half-acre of terraced garden was a 'sprouting jungle' (pp. 130–1). The cottage, complete with 'a pump and apple trees, syringa and strawberries, rooks in the chimneys, frogs in the cellar, mushrooms on the ceiling' (p. 10), stood on a steep bank sloping down to a lake, where swans settled in the summer (pp. 148–9). The stone house was 'handsome as they go', according to Lee, with 'hand-carved windows, golden surfaces, moss-flaked tiles', and damp, thick walls (p. 78).

The twenty to thirty other cottages of the village were similarly made of grey Cotswold stone; their split-stone roofs gleamed with golden moss. Scattered on the south-east slope of Slad valley, they had 'long steep gardens full of cabbages, fruit-bushes, roses, rabbit-hutches, earth-closets, bicycles, and pigeon-lofts'. Low in the valley and larger than these was the Big House, a 'fine, though modest sixteenth-century manor, to which a Georgian facade had been added' (p. 42). Lee describes the musty, tapestried interior—as seen from the door by the gaping choirboys—in 'Winter and Summer' (p. 144); he describes the long drive and beech woods, the lake and gardens in 'Outings and Festivals' (pp. 186–7).

In addition to these homes, the village boasted a church and a chapel, the vicarage and a manse, the village school, Vick's shop, and a pub (p. 42). Nearby was Jones's pond, a place of lush growth in the summer (p. 151), used for ice-skating in winter (pp. 140–1), and chosen by Miss Flynn for suicide (pp. 101–4). At the edge of the village lay Farmer Wells's land. The slopes of the valley made good pasturage; the tops of the hills, as described in 'Village School', were covered with beechwoods. Locked in the steep, narrow valley, often in winter the village was cut off, isolated by snow.

The nearest town was Stroud; the valley was one of 'Stroud's five valleys' (p. 68). Four miles away was Sheepscombe; in the next valley, visible from the high saddle of land known as Bulls Cross, was Painswick, described in 'Outings and Festivals' as a 'starfish of light dilating in a pool of distance' (p. 188) at night, and a white, sprawled 'skeleton of a foundered mammoth' by day (p. 190). Bulls Cross itself, a high wind-swept heathland at the end of the valley, was 'once a crossing of stage-roads and cattle-tracks which joined Berkeley to Birdlip, and Bisley to Gloucester-Market' (p. 32). It overlooked the dark wood known as Deadcombe Bottom, where could be found the decaying ruin of Hangman's House.

The social structure of the village

Lee indicates the social structure of the village in 'Last Days' by describing the rigid seating arrangement in church:

> The leading benches contained our gentry, their pews marked with visiting cards: the Lords of the Manor, Squire Jones and the Croomes; then the Army, the Carvossos and Dovetons; the rich

and settled spinsters, the Misses Abels and Bagnalls; and finally the wealthier farmers. All were neatly arranged by protocol, with the Squire up front by the pulpit (p. 219).

In 'Winter and Summer', he describes the boys of the Choir, carolling up and down the valley, 'visiting the lesser and the greater gentry— the farmers, the doctors, the merchants, the majors, and other exalted persons' (p. 146). At the houses of the gentry, Laurie caught glimpses of wealth, but he was never invited to enter: 'we sang in courtyards and porches, outside windows, or in the damp gloom of hallways; . . . we smelt rich clothes and strange hot food; we saw maids bearing in dishes or carrying away coffee-cups,' . . . we sang as it were at the castle walls' (p. 146).

Lee's faint irony expresses little or no indignation; his portrait, for example, of the tottering, wet-eyed Squire, perpetually delivering short opening speeches and passing out awards, is always affectionate, if wry. 'The Squire was our centre', he acknowledges, 'a crumbling moot tree; and few indeed of our local celebrations could take place without his shade' (p. 184). The authority of the Squire was still accepted unquestioningly, for during Lee's boyhood, the village still was poised between the feudal past and the industrial future; Lee states that the general run of villagers 'had three ways of living: working for the Squire, or on the farms, or down in the cloth-mills at Stroud' (p. 42). Only once does he record a dissenting voice, that of Vincent, in 'Public Death, Private Murder', who returns home newly rich to taunt the villagers:

> They slogged for the Squire and the tenant-farmers for a miserable twelve bob a week. They lived on potatoes and by touching their caps, they hadn't a sovereign to rub between them, they saw not a thing save muck and each other—and perhaps Stroud on a Saturday night (p. 96).

For expressing this view, more than for his money and gold watch, Vincent is set upon by angry village youths and then left to freeze to death in the snow.

Basic economic conditions in the village: food, clothing, shelter

A few in the village were wealthy, but Mrs Lee's family and friends were not of them. She herself dished up bacon and greens while remembering elaborate meals in the homes of the gentry. In *Cider with Rosie*, old Mrs Davies boils up a pot of gruel; Granny Trill lives on tea, biscuits, and presents of porridge; Granny Wallon lives on 'cabbage, bread, and potatoes' (p. 79); the gipsy schoolboy Rosso steals his food because he does not have enough; the old Brown couple are known for 'a little foraging, some frugal feeding' (p. 109). Breakfast in the Lee house is 'smoky lumps with treacle', tea and sugared bread (p. 67); the evening meal might be pancakes or lentil stew, 'a heavy brown mash made apparently of plastic studs' (p. 69). The family daily devoured eight loaves of delivered bread, their monotony lightened, Lee observes, 'by the objects we found in them—string, nails, paper, and once a mouse' (p. 16). Lee lists in 'First Light' the abundant vegetables the family enjoyed during the summer (pp. 15–16), and in 'Outings and Festivals' he describes going to the wild reaches of the valley to gather fruit (p. 188). But there was never enough meat: 'sometimes a pound of bare ribs for boiling, or an occasional rabbit dumped at the door by a neighbour' (p. 16). In 'The Kitchen', Lee remembers, 'we were always hungry . . . the size of our family outstripped the size of the pot, so there was never quite enough to go round' (pp. 68–9). Ruefully recalling futile races with Jack for the dregs of the stew-pot, Lee allows himself a rare complaint: 'it left me marked with an ugly scar, a twisted, food-crazed nature, so that still I am calling for whole rice puddings and big pots of stew in the night' (pp. 69–70).

Lee pays little attention to clothing; as all were dressed similarly, the village children did not notice they were dressed neither well nor warmly. In 'Village School', four-year-old Laurie, encircled on arrival, sees at eye-level 'old boots, ragged stockings, torn trousers and skirts' (p. 43); Lee later describes a few of his schoolmates as a 'straggle of long-faced children, pinched, solemn, raggedly dressed' (p. 57). Thickly wrapped in scarves, in winter the children wear old army puttees and carry old cocoa tins punched with holes and packed with smouldering rags to keep their hands warm (p. 137). Lee includes these details without dwelling upon them. Instead he delights in the ingenuity of the villagers in creating the cocoa tin hand-warmers and sewing festive costumes. He praises the 'patchwork glories' put together by his sisters: 'it was remarkable what raiment they managed to conjure considering what little they had' (p. 89). But Lee's greatest enthusiasm is reserved for the 'high laced boots and long muslin dresses, beaded chokers and candlewick shawls, crowned by tall poke bonnets tied with trailing ribbons and smothered with inky sequins', all worn by the grannies (p. 87).

The Cotswold stone houses were old, very beautiful, and very damp; Lee recalls the thick walls 'kept a damp chill inside them whatever the season or weather' (p. 78). Lighted by candle and paraffin lamp, the kitchens became inviting caves at night; unheated except in times of sickness, the upper bedrooms were icy cold in winter. In the Lee family, 'wash-basins could freeze, icicles hang from the ornaments, our bedrooms remained normally unheated; but the lighting of a fire . . . meant that serious illness had come' (p. 158). Old Mr Davies, in fact, spent his last illness in an 'ice-cold poky bedroom' (p. 107). 'Winter . . . was the worst time for the old ones' Lee reports in 'Public Death, Private Murder' (p. 106); in 'Sick Boy', he states that high infant mortality also was taken for granted: 'Those were the days, . . . when children faded quickly, when there was little to be done, should the lungs be affected, but to burn coal-tar and pray. In those cold valley cottages, with their dripping walls, damp beds, and oozing floors, a child could sicken and die in a year' (p. 167).

Lee's focus is on the pleasure of his growing up; he does not emphasise his family's poverty nor the general hardships of living in his time and village. But neither does he falsify his record. Always he dwells on the light and hints at the dark; the resulting shadow gives to his village portrait an added depth.

Village ways

To live in the village was to be isolated. In summer its 'untarred road wound . . . empty away to other villages . . . waiting for the sight of a stranger' (p. 150); in winter the villagers expected that drifting snow would often cut them off from the rest of the world. 'Like an island', Lee remembers, the valley 'was possessed of curious survivals—rare orchids and Roman snails' (p. 41), but the remoteness was more than physical. 'The village was the world and its happenings all I knew', he recalls (p. 104); when he and his brothers seized Granny Trill's almanac, they saw in its ominous illustrations 'the whole outside world, split, convulsive, and damned'. But, he adds, 'It had nothing, of course, to do with our village' (p. 85).

Literally, then, a world unto itself, the village often lived outside the law. The villagers fed a deserter from the army until he was hunted down by the police and taken away in a cart (pp. 19–20). When murder was committed in the village, police again came, but 'their inquiries were met by stares' (p. 97); even now, upon telling the story, Lee hastens to add protectively that the murderers 'are all of them dead now anyway' (p. 98). Elsewhere he says that the villagers possessed a 'frank and unfearful attitude to death, and an acceptance of violence as a kind of ritual which no one accused or pardoned' (p. 105). He explains further in a short essay inserted in 'Public Death, Private Murder', 'We knew ourselves to be as corrupt as any other community of our size—as any London street, for instance. But . . . transgressors were dealt with by local opinion, by silence, lampoons, or nicknames' (p. 205). The villagers were tolerant towards crimes of violence, such as rape, manslaughter, murder, and towards those against property, such as robbery and arson. They merely laughed at the sexual experimentation of youth, and were aware that 'quiet incest flourished where the roads were bad; some found their comfort in beasts; and there were the usual friendships between men and boys who walked through the fields like lovers'. In all these cases, Lee states, 'the village neither approved nor disapproved, but neither did it complain to authority' (p. 206).

The villagers were tolerant of the violent or sexual actions of those it considered its own. The offspring of the incestuous John-Jack and his sister were never ostracised (p. 57). Those who attempted or committed suicide 'were never censured, but were spoken about in a special voice as though their actions raised them above the living and defeated the misery of the world' (p. 108). The young men who murdered Vincent 'were not treated as outcasts, nor did they appear to live under any special stain', for 'they belonged to the village and the village looked after them' (p. 98).

The villagers, however, were intolerant of outsiders, setting their dogs upon wandering gipsies (p. 58). They were particularly suspicious of those among them who, like the hapless Vincent, had become different in some way. Credulity and superstition were partly responsible for this attitude. Fred Bates, for example, had been one of them, but after he came upon Miss Flynn's body and saw the dead man in Stroud, the superstitious villagers took away his milk round, refused to look him in the eye, and crossed the road to avoid him (p. 104). With unthinking cruelty, they denied the deaf-mute beggar called Albert the Devil the chance to encounter another human being; as he was thought to have unusual powers as well as unusual eyes, when the villagers heard 'his musical gurgle approaching, money and food was put on the tops of the walls and then people shut themselves up in their privies' (p. 35).

A record of the passing of a way of life

Remnants of the past in the present

Growing up in the early part of the twentieth century in a Cotswold village, Laurie Lee was aware of traces of the very distant past still surviving in the land and memories of the villagers. 'There were ghosts in the stones, in the trees, and the walls, and each field and hill had several', he writes; 'there were certain landmarks about the valley—tree-clumps, corners in the woods—that bore separate, antique, half-muttered names that were certainly older than Christian' (p. 105). Tragic occurrences were recalled in the stories and superstitions of the villagers. Thus in 'First Names' Lee describes the phantom of the Bulls Cross Coach, its coachman, passengers and terrified horses regularly re-enacting at midnight a fatal accident; its last run, Lee states, 'had been jealously remembered to haunt us' (p. 33). He shows us the first step in this process in 'Public Death, Private Murder', when he recounts the story of Miss Flynn's suicide. He and other villagers stood gaping the next morning at the very spot where she died, trying to visualise exactly what had happened, and Lee asserts, 'for me, as long as I can remember, Miss Flynn remained drowned in that pond' (p. 104).

The villagers' uninterrupted contact with the long centuries of their continuous past was revealed not only in their stories and superstitions, but in their genealogy and their way of life. Recalling a harvest Sunday in 'Outings and Festivals', Lee says the villagers justly gathered to praise 'pride, placation, and the continuity of growth', for 'the seed of these fruits, and the seed of these men, still came from the same one bowl; confined to this valley and renewing itself here, it went back to the days of the Ice' (p. 221). The elegaic paragraphs which begin 'Last Days' tell us how even the daily routine of the villagers' lives went back at least a thousand years: 'Myself, my family, my generation, were born in a world . . . of hard work and necessary patience, of backs bent to the ground, hands massaging the crops, of waiting on weather and growth.' The restrictions of their ancestors were still theirs: the horse's 'eight miles an hour was the limit of our movements, as it had been since the days of the Romans' (p. 217).

Apparently young Laurie's imagination frequently made him aware of present resemblances to the prehistoric past, and Lee's metaphors refer more often to the Ice Age than to the Romans. Describing the family gathered round their stove in 'The Kitchen', Lee asserts that 'the state of our fire became as important . . . as it must have been to a primitive tribe', and that when the fire went out it seemed that 'winter had come for ever, that the wolves of the wilderness were gathering near' (p. 72). In 'Winter and Summer', he describes gathering sticks at night in a wood 'silent and freezing hard, white and smelling of wolves'. It was, he exclaims, 'such a night as lost hunters must have stared upon when they wandered north into the Ice Age' (p. 141). In the middle of 'Public Death, Private Murder', in an extraordinary extended simile, Lee expresses his sense of the village's continuity from the time of great glaciers, comparing the village to a 'deep-running cave' which 'had not, as yet, been tidied up, or scrubbed clean by electric light, or suburbanized by a Victorian church, or papered by cinema screens' (p. 104).

The present becoming the past

Lee is characteristically nostalgic. In 'Winter and Summer' he describes feeding Farmer Wells's livestock an ordinary fodder 'with grass and wild flowers juicily fossilized within—a whole summer embalmed in our arms' (p. 139). In 'Grannies in the Wainscot', he describes seasons fermenting and summers boiling in Granny Wallon's vats, and recalls that her wine preserved the fragrance of 'ripe grass in some far-away field' (p. 80). To Lee, in 'The Uncles', the five Light brothers embodied the passing life of an entire nation; their lives spoke the 'long farewell' of an earlier age, and 'spoke, too, of campaigns on desert marches, of Kruger's cannon, and Flanders mud; of a world that still moved at the same pace as Caesar's, and of that Empire greater than his—through which they had fought, sharp-eyed and anonymous, and seen the first outposts crumble . . .' (p. 183). The preserving in some manner of what once existed matters to Lee; and so does the recording of its passing. Thus in 'Last Days', Lee chronicles the major changes which occurred in his tiny Cotswold village.

Structure and style

Narrative structure

'Technically the book was not so simple', states Lee of his work on *Cider with Rosie* in his essay 'Writing Biography' *(I Can't Stay Long)*. 'It took two years and was written three times.' A major part of his technical problem was the structure: 'If a book is to stand, one must first choose its shape—the house that the tale will inhabit.' Lee's book is ordered only roughly by chronology. It begins when he is three and for the first time set down in the tall grass of the village; it ends when he is in late adolescence and getting ready to leave the village (the next autobiographical volume, *As I Walked Out One Midsummer Morning*, begins with that leave-taking and a final glimpse of his mother, standing waist-deep in that same tall grass as she waves good-bye). Chronology, usually adhered to in autobiographies, is not strict in *Cider with Rosie*. In the seventh chapter, 'Mother', for example, Lee describes a few hours from his years during the Second World War; two chapters later, in 'Sick Boy', he spends several pages upon his infancy. Moreover, no exciting plot—a sequence of events governed by cause and effect within a narrative—holds Lee's book together, other than the facts that Laurie grows up and the village changes.

Individual chapters, then, deal with themes. When Lee began to write *Cider with Rosie*, he saw his early life in the village as 'a great landscape darkly fogged by the years and thickly matted by rumour and legend. . . . gradually . . . memory began to stir, setting off flash-points like summer lightning' ('Writing Autobiography'). He wrote an episode around each small illumination, and grouped series of episodes around general themes. Thus there are chapters devoted to village celebrations, memorable deaths, village wonders, sexual initiation, and so on. He himself calls this manner of writing 'episodic and momentarily revealing'. Occasionally the chapters are even disassociated to the extent that information given in one does not fit with that given in the others, as when, for example, Lee speaks in 'The Uncles' of 'the satiny bodies of my younger brothers and sisters' (p. 174). Throughout the rest of the book he has only one younger brother and one younger sister, who died. Such flaws, however, occur only rarely.

The order of these thematic chapters, in addition to being very roughly chronological, is spatial; it corresponds to young Laurie's widening exploration of his world. Even within chapters this principle is often followed, so that in 'First Light', for example, Lee shows himself at three adventurously moving outward 'from stone to stone in the trackless yard' (p. 14). In 'Writing Autobiography', Lee describes how his young self 'ruled as king' the early chapters of *Cider with Rosie* and how later chapters included more and more of the outside world: 'the book moved away from me—taking in first my family, then our house and the village, and finally the whole of the valley'.

One other structual device might be noted here: compression. Lee wished his episodes, his illuminations, to serve as 'small beacons to mark the peaks of the story and to accentuate the darkness of what was left out' ('Writing Autobiography'). Only rarely, as in the half-sisters' visit in their finery to indignant Granny Trill, and in the village celebration of Peace Day, do readers have the sense that actions being described occurred only once. Instead, Lee is clearly concerned with habitual action, a long childhood of familiar routine and a village life of patterns well established over past centuries. Thus in 'Outings and Festivals', he re-creates a typical yearly Parochia! Church Tea and Annual Entertainment and describes a representative annual Choir Outing. In 'The Kitchen', he shows a typical day within the household; as this chapter is concerned with family life, he focuses it mainly upon the times during the day when they are all together (pp. 65–77). Lee shows two other typical days from morning to night in 'Winter and Summer'; as his concern here is to present 'village-winter or village-summer, both separate', all the events of the first day are typical of winter (pp. 136–42), and all those of the second typical of summer (pp. 148–54). Finally, in 'Last Days', Lee shows a typical Sunday, distinguished from weekdays by 'being a combination of both indulgence and discipline' (pp. 218–20). His accounts of these four days, representative of all the weekdays and Sundays, winter days and summer days of his boyhood, each begin with Laurie's waking or stumbling downstairs to the kitchen; they proceed chronologically through the day, hour by hour, until evening.

Finally, it is clear that Lee had to place some material in certain chapters arbitrarily. The carolling of the Choir at Christmas, for example, is placed alongside other winter activities in 'Winter and Summer', rather than next to the singing of the Choir at Matins and Evensong in 'Last Days'. Again comparing the structure of a book such as *Cider with Rosie* to the structure of a house, Lee describes in 'Writing Autobiography' how 'one lays out the rooms for the necessary chapters', and begins 'pacing the empty rooms, knowing that what goes in there can belong nowhere else'.

Point of view

As is customary in such self-portraits, Lee's autobiography is told in the first person. The use of that 'I'—which in autobiographies refers to central character, narrator, and author alike—is less egocentric than is often the case, however, for Lee spends less time than is spent in most autobiographies looking inward and outward. Even when he is dealing with the self-absorption of an infant, for example, he prefers to work not by focusing directly on himself as a baby, but by focusing on the marvellous properties of water, as seen through his three-year-old eyes. Later, of course, when Lee makes the 'I' within *Cider with Rosie* 'less a character than a presence, a listening shadow', he shifts from the 'I' as protagonist to the 'I' as witness.

Often more concerned with other villagers, Lee includes within his autobiographical narrative several brief stories of other people's lives. If lifted from the pages of *Cider with Rosie* these stories would be complete in themselves, although only a few paragraphs long. The central characters of these stories—such as the delightful Blacksmith and Toffee-Maker, for example—are obviously not the narrator; the stories are told in the third person: 'He proposed, and they married, and lived forever contented, and used his forge for boiling their toffee' (p. 133).

Occasionally, however, Lee writes even these small complete stories of other lives in the first person, but within dialogue; he usually does this when he wants to reveal character through speech pattern, selection, and emphasis. Two examples of this variation occur in 'Mother' where Lee retells in his mother's own words her stories of the Indian prince and the privy and of the regimental 'Eyes right!' (pp. 116–19).

Characterisation

Lee uses several methods of characterisation in creating his portraits of family members and other villagers. He uses dialogue frequently and effectively. Lee shows his villagers' characteristic way of speaking in mere snatches, so that every word must ring true. Granny Trill's 'I still got me bits', Miss Flynn's 'I've been bad, Mrs Er', and Bet's 'Gis a wine-gum, and I'll show ya, if ya want'—each of these statements seems to sum up the character in a line. The problems of such selection and compression became more acute in creating dialogue for those more close to Lee. As he remarks in 'Writing Autobiography', 'The flowing chatter of my sisters, for twelve years unstaunched, had to be distilled to a few dozen phrases—phrases, perhaps which they had never quite uttered, but bearing the accents of all that they had'. Occasionally Lee allows his characters to speak at greater length, telling their own stories in their own words, and when his story tellers thus select and arrange moments from their past they are also revealing characteristic ways of thinking.

In addition to using dialogue, Lee employs action to characterise villagers, and the typical reaction this causes in others. Cabbage-Stump Charlie, for example, is portrayed in this manner:

> He would set out each evening, armed with his cabbage-stalk, ready to strike down the first man he saw. . . . Men fell from their bicycles or back-pedalled violently when they saw old Charlie coming . . . he would take up his stand outside the pub, swing his great stump round his head, and say 'Wham! Bash!' like a boy in a comic, and challenge all comers to battle. (p. 35)

Economical in creating a minor character, this method is also effective in adding to the portrait of a major character. Thus Lee shows his mother working over the stove in the kitchen, poking under the piano for her corsets, riding her bicycle out of control down a hill, filling various jars and pots with flowers, playing the piano at night, alone in her finery, and so on.

In portraying both minor and major characters, Lee frequently writes set pieces of physical description. Thus Albert the Devil, who has 'soft-boiled eyes', is first described as 'a deaf-mute beggar with a black beetle's body, short legs, and a mouth like a puppet's' (p. 35). Marjorie, 'a blonde Aphrodite', is described as 'tall, long-haired, and dreamily gentle, and her voice was low and slow' (p. 61). However, as even these examples show, Lee finds it difficult to confine himself merely to factual phrases (deaf-mute, short legs, long-haired) in writing physical descriptions.

Thus, throughout *Cider with Rosie*, Lee employs the various poetic means of comparison known as figures of speech to convey the look or essence of a character. In the above examples, he uses allusion (Aphrodite), simile (like a puppet's) and metaphor (a black beetle's body). Using metaphor, he describes Granny Wallon as 'a tiny white shrew who came nibbling through her garden, who clawed squeaking with gossip at our kitchen window, or sat sucking bread in the sun' (p. 78). Using simile, Lee says Fred Bates had a 'head like a bottle-brush' (p. 100) and young Jo a body 'pale and milk-green on the grass, like a birch-leaf lying in water, slightly curved like a leaf and veined and glowing, lit faintly from within its flesh' (p. 204). Often Lee creates a beautiful extended metaphor or simile, such as this one, in which he describes Granny Trill: 'Like a delicate pale bubble, blown a little higher and further than the other girls of her generation, she had floated just long enough for us to catch sight of her . . .' (p. 92).

Style

Two conspicuous aspects of Lee's style are his use of irony and his use of the poetic resources of the language—both figures of speech (such as metaphor, simile, personification, allusion) and devices of sound (such as assonance, consonance, alliteration, rhyme).

Irony implies a discrepancy of some sort. In 'verbal irony', often defined as saying the opposite of what is meant, the discrepancy occurs between the words used and the actual meaning. Clearly Lee does not feel that a Conservative victory is reason for the entire nation—or all villagers—to rejoice (or at least he does not consider winning an election and winning a war to be equally important events); thus he uses irony when he describes the Squire as follows: 'On the greater occasions he let us loose in his gardens, on the smaller gave us buns and speeches; and at historic moments of national rejoicing—when kings were born, enemies vanquished, or the Conservatives won an election—he ransacked his boxrooms for fancy-dresses that we might rejoice in a proper manner' (p. 184). Characteristically, Lee's use of irony results in economy of prose, for in one side-long phrase, Lee exposes the Squire's assumptions about the villagers' political beliefs, hints at his slightly befuddled sense of the relative value of things, and indicates the scarcity of Conservative victories. Lee's descriptions of the Squire are ironic, but not sarcastic. His use of irony here is not meant to wound. Lee comes closest to sarcasm when he describes his father; his use of irony then is a little darker, a little bitter: 'The First World War gave him the chance he wanted, and though properly distrustful of arms and battle he instantly sacrificed both himself and his family, applied for a post in the Army Pay Corps, went off to Greenwich in a bullet-proof vest, and never permanently lived with us again' (pp. 60–1). Lee uses verbal irony when he observes that his father 'sacrificed' himself by deserting his family and accepting a good-paying job. The discrepancy implied by 'chance' and 'bullet-proof' is of a different sort, however. Readers do not expect a tragic war to be viewed as opportunity; they do not expect protection from flying bullets to be necessary in quiet towns so close to London.

Lee uses this kind of irony again when he describes the fire at the boiler-works: 'The warehouse, as usual, was sheathed in flame, ceilings and floors fell in, firemen shouted, windows melted like icicles, and from inside the building one heard thundering booms as the boilers started crashing about' (p. 224). Readers scarcely expect the list of details Lee gives to follow the mundane phrase, 'as usual', but Lee really means it, for the boiler-works fire occurred so frequently it was almost an anticipated annual local event. In this case the discrepancy is between what is expected by the reader and what actually occurs, and is known as 'irony of situation'.

In writing prose, Lee uses many of the devices of poetry. Frequently his sentences fall into rhythmic cadences: 'Proud in the night the beast passed by' (p. 30). At times they slip into rising regularity: 'her hair was rich as a wild bee's nest and her eyes were full of stings' (p. 209). Occasionally he rhymes: 'We kissed, once only, so dry and shy' (p. 210). He uses assonance, choosing words in which vowel sounds repeat: 'dusty with buttercups'. And he uses alliteration, choosing words with repeating initial or internal consonants: 'rabbits jumped like firecrackers about the field' (p. 208). But as even this last line shows, what most distinguishes Lee's vivid prose is the poet's constant use of freshly created figures of speech: feeding a calf; he 'opened its mouth like a hot wet orchid' (p. 139); 'the sun hit me smartly on the face, like a bully', he wrote earlier (p. 9).

Sometimes, for the reasons mentioned above, Lee uses his similes and metaphors to communicate the essence of his characters, to convey something that could not be said in factual language: 'bard and oracles each', the uncles were 'like a ring of squat megaliths on some local hill, bruised by weather and scarred with old glories' (p. 183). Particularly in the early chapters, when Laurie is a small boy exploring a large world, Lee uses his poetic language to create a sense of adventure. In the following passage, for example, the grass becomes a jungle terrifyingly concealing strange animals and sharp weapons:

It towered above me and all round me, each blade tattooed with tiger-skins of sunlight. It was knife-edged, dark, and a wicked green, thick as a forest and alive with grasshoppers that chirped and chattered and leapt through the air like monkeys (p. 9).

When Laurie learns about water in the scullery, the humble room becomes the high seas of boyish adventure, and his mother and sisters become tall ships before the wind:

> From the harbour mouth of the scullery door I learned the rocks and reefs and the channels where safety lay. . . . My Mother and sisters sailed past me like galleons in their busy dresses, and I learned the smells and sounds which followed in their wakes . . . How magnificent they appeared, full-rigged, those towering girls, with their flying hair and billowing blouses, their white-mast arms stripped for work or washing (pp. 14–15).

Thus Lee frequently transforms the ordinary into the extraordinary; he writes prose like the poet he is.

Part 4

Hints for study

Selection of material

The student will find it helpful to know basic critical terms and to be able to apply them. These terms include: 'theme', 'point of view', 'setting', 'structure', 'summary', 'scene', 'character', and 'style'.

Theme

The central idea or insight presented in a literary work is called its 'theme'. Summed up in a single sentence, the theme is stated in general rather than specific terms; different readers will naturally use different phrasing. The theme of *Cider with Rosie* might be stated as follows: Growing up in a small village in the 1920s acquainted Cotswold children with a simple, traditional, but enjoyable life, now for ever lost.

Point of view

'Point of view' refers to the perspective from which a story is told, or the eyes through which the action is seen; thus it requires identifying the narrator of a literary work (often distinct from its author), and describing both his part in the action and the limitations of his knowledge. The narrator may use first person (I) or third person (he, she, it, they); he may be a participant or non-participant in the action; he may know everything or be limited in knowledge. (See Part 3, Point of view, p. 50.)

Setting

'Setting' refers to the time and place of a story. In *Cider with Rosie*, the setting is a small village in the Cotswolds in western England between 1918 and 1930.

Structure

'Structure' refers to the way the major parts of a work are put together: the framework of a narrative, its construction, shaping, and ordering. *Cider with Rosie*, briefly, has thirteen chapters which are ordered chronologically and spatially; each chapter is divided into smaller sections which are grouped thematically. (See Part 3, Narrative structure, pp. 48–50.)

Summary and scene

In writing a narrative, an author must constantly decide between telling what happened and showing it. If the action occurs over a long period of time, or is repetitive, or of lesser significance, he will summarise in general, economical statements: 'He settled then in the local forests and became one of the best woodsmen in the Cotswolds' (p. 171). This is 'summary'. If the event is a major one, the author will show the moment dramatically, using dialogue and detail to recreate it vividly: '"I'm old Granny Trill, a-eating her dinner", said Jack, sucking peel through his gums' (p. 89). This closer, detailed description constitutes a 'scene'.

Character

The imagined or remembered people portrayed in a narrative are its 'characters'. A 'round' character is many-faceted and gradually changes from page to page; a 'flat' character has one or two familiar traits and changes little or not at all. In *Cider with Rosie*, Mrs Lee is a round character; Cabbage-Stump Charlie is a flat character. (For further commentary, see Part 3, Characterisation, pp. 51–2. For commentary on individual characters, see Part 3, pp. 30–41.

Style

Included under 'style' are the many aspects of an author's writing which make his work unique: his choice of words; his characteristic use of imagery, poetic figures of speech, and patterns of sound; the usual length and pattern of his sentences. (See Part 3, Style, pp. 52–4.)

Organisation of material

Students of literature, particularly when quickly constructing examination answers, will find it convenient to know basic patterns of paragraph organisation. Two of the most frequently used paragraph patterns are (*a*) the paragraph of thesis and support, and (*b*) the paragraph of comparison or contrast.

Paragraph of thesis and support

The first sentence of a thesis and support paragraph states a claim: the writer asserts something. The value of the paragraph will rest in part upon the value of the claim, so it should not be trivial. The rest of the paragraph (the 'body') will offer material supporting the claim—perhaps two short examples and one extended example, perhaps a list of significant details, perhaps a series of reasons illustrated by references to the text. A claim may have several parts; if so, each part should be taken up in turn in a sentence of its own and support given.

When speaking or writing about a literary work, it is best to remember the primary evidence is the text. Specific references to the text and selected quotations from it will both illustrate and prove your major points. (See paragraphs 2–6 of the section on Laurie's mother in Part 3, pp. 30–2, for examples of thesis and support using selected quotations and specific references to the text.)

Paragraph of comparison or contrast

The paragraph of comparison or contrast points out similarities or differences between two items. The value of the paragraph will rest in part upon the significance of these similarities or differences; the comparison or contrast should not be written idly, but should have a purpose. Thus the first sentence should indicate not only what comparison or contrast is to be made, but its significance. In the body of such a paragraph, equivalent information must be given about each item. Each item may be taken up in turn, with the same points covered in the same order for each (Item A, points 1, 2, 3; Item B, points 1, 2, 3). Alternatively, the paragraph may be ordered point by point (Point 1, items A, B; Point 2, items A, B; Point 3, items A, B). In either case, balance is essential.

A sample paragraph of thesis and support

QUESTION: *What principles of organisation has Lee used in* Cider with Rosie?

The structure of *Cider with Rosie* is complex, for Laurie Lee has ordered his autobiography by topic, time, and space. He constructs a chapter by grouping smaller units which deal with the same theme. Thus individual chapters are focused upon school (Chapter 3), old neighbours (Chapter 5), Lee's mother (Chapter 7), childhood illness (Chapter 9), and so on. In addition, he often orders the sections within a chapter chronologically. Chapter 3, 'Village School', for example, moves from the first day of school to Laurie's stay in Infants, through the years in the Big Room, to the last day of school. The reader experiences things roughly in the order in which the growing Laurie encountered them. Thus the overall order of the thirteen chapters of the book is chronological. The three-year-old's elemental exploration of water and earth in 'First Light' is placed at the beginning of the narrative, Chapter 1; the chapter focusing on the adolescent's sexual awakening is placed near the end of the narrative, Chapter 12. The overall order of the book is also spatial: as Laurie explores his physical environment, the action of the book occurs over a wider and wider space. Thus adventures in the cottage and back yard are placed at the start, Chapter 1. The gradual explorations of village and valley occupy the middle chapters. Annual Outings allow Laurie to burst free of the confines of the valley, so 'Outings and Festivals' is placed near the end, Chapter 11. Information that Laurie's world is grown even larger is given in Chapter 13: 'The sun and moon, which once rose from our hill, rose from London now in the east.'

A sample paragraph of contrast

QUESTION: *How did the village change during Lee's childhood and adolescence?*

Reflecting the general movement toward modernisation which occurred in the world during the first decades of the twentieth century, the village of Laurie Lee's late adolescence differed significantly from the village he had known in childhood. The village roads in the late 1920s, when the change occurred in the village, became busy places of motor-cars and charabancs; the roads in Lee's childhood had been still, the dust never stirring during long summer hours, the deep snow often making them impassable during long winter months. Then, at best, travel had been limited by the horse's eight miles an hour; in the 1920s, distances became closer and people travelled easily to nearby towns. There, the visiting villagers saw films in the new picture palaces, and at home news of the outside world came by radio. Finding entertainment ready-made outside the village, the newly restless villagers would never again be completely content—as they had been—with only the entertainment they fashioned for themselves: their own songs and music, the Parochial Church Tea and Annual Entertainment, conversation around a winter fire. Thus the pervading silence and isolation of the village Laurie had known as a child was broken, and the village's self-sufficiency for ever altered. Other changes also occurred. The village of Laurie's childhood had been a close-knit community, held together by an unquestioning acceptance of the joint authority of church and Squire. That cohesive centre did not hold after the 1920s, when the vicar retired and the Squire died. With the power of the church everywhere greatly lessened and lingering feudal relationships for ever gone, villagers no longer enjoyed a way of life their families had known for centuries. They scattered, and the village, as Lee writes in 'Last Days', became 'no more than a place for pensioners'.

Part 5

Suggestions for
further reading

The text

The text used in the preparation of these Notes is: Laurie Lee, *Cider with Rosie*, Penguin Books, Harmondsworth, 1962. This paperback edition is published in the U.S.A. by Viking Penguin, New York.

Other works by Laurie Lee

As I Walked Out One Midsummer Morning, Penguin Books, Harmondsworth, 1969.
The Bloom of Candles, Lehmann, London, 1947.
The Firstborn, Hogarth Press, London, 1964.
I Can't Stay Long, Penguin Books, Harmondsworth, 1975.
My Many-Coated Man, André Deutsch, London, 1955.
A Rose for Winter, Hogarth Press, London, 1961.
The Sun My Monument, Hogarth Press, London, 1944.
The Voyage of Magellan, Lehmann, London, 1947.

General reading

ANDERSON, SHERWOOD: *Winesburg, Ohio*, Penguin Books, Harmondsworth, 1976.
LAWRENCE, D. H.: *Sons and Lovers*, Penguin Books, Harmondsworth, 1969.
MASTERS, EDGAR LEE: *Spoon River Anthology*, Collier-Macmillan, West Drayton, 1962.
The Poetical Works of Wordsworth, edited by Thomas Hutchinson, second edition, revised by Ernest de Selincourt, Oxford University Press, London, 1960.
THOMAS, DYLAN: *Under Milk Wood*, Dent, London, 1954.
WILDER, THORNTON: *Our Town*, Longman, Harlow, 1964.

The author of these notes

Born in Wisconsin, Jean Tobin has lived in Virginia, Michigan and New York, and in Boston, Paris, Edinburgh and the Lake District in England. She was educated at the University of Wisconsin at Madison, and has taught contemporary literature at Luther College and the University of Wisconsin at Green Bay. She now teaches at the University of Wisconsin Center at Sheboygan.

York Notes: list of titles

CHINUA ACHEBE
Things Fall Apart
EDWARD ALBEE
Who's Afraid of Virginia Woolf?
ANONYMOUS
Beowulf
Everyman
W. H. AUDEN
Selected Poems
JANE AUSTEN
Emma
Mansfield Park
Northanger Abbey
Persuasion
Pride and Prejudice
Sense and Sensibility
SAMUEL BECKETT
Waiting for Godot
ARNOLD BENNETT
The Card
JOHN BETJEMAN
Selected Poems
WILLIAM BLAKE
Songs of Innocence, Songs of Experience
ROBERT BOLT
A Man For All Seasons
HAROLD BRIGHOUSE
Hobson's Choice
ANNE BRONTË
The Tenant of Wildfell Hall
CHARLOTTE BRONTË
Jane Eyre
EMILY BRONTË
Wuthering Heights
ROBERT BROWNING
Men and Women
JOHN BUCHAN
The Thirty-Nine Steps
JOHN BUNYAN
The Pilgrim's Progress
BYRON
Selected Poems
GEOFFREY CHAUCER
Prologue to the Canterbury Tales
The Clerk's Tale
The Franklin's Tale
The Knight's Tale
The Merchant's Tale
The Miller's Tale
The Nun's Priest's Tale

The Pardoner's Tale
The Wife of Bath's Tale
Troilus and Criseyde
SAMUEL TAYLOR COLERIDGE
Selected Poems
SIR ARTHUR CONAN DOYLE
The Hound of the Baskervilles
WILLIAM CONGREVE
The Way of the World
JOSEPH CONRAD
Heart of Darkness
STEPHEN CRANE
The Red Badge of Courage
BRUCE DAWE
Selected Poems
DANIEL DEFOE
Moll Flanders
Robinson Crusoe
WALTER DE LA MARE
Selected Poems
SHELAGH DELANEY
A Taste of Honey
CHARLES DICKENS
A Tale of Two Cities
Bleak House
David Copperfield
Great Expectations
Hard Times
Oliver Twist
The Pickwick Papers
EMILY DICKINSON
Selected Poems
JOHN DONNE
Selected Poems
GERALD DURRELL
My Family and Other Animals
GEORGE ELIOT
Middlemarch
Silas Marner
The Mill on the Floss
T. S. ELIOT
Four Quartets
Murder in the Cathedral
Selected Poems
The Cocktail Party
The Waste Land
J. G. FARRELL
The Siege of Krishnapur
WILLIAM FAULKNER
The Sound and the Fury

HENRY FIELDING
Joseph Andrews
Tom Jones
F. SCOTT FITZGERALD
Tender is the Night
The Great Gatsby
GUSTAVE FLAUBERT
Madame Bovary
E. M. FORSTER
A Passage to India
Howards End
JOHN FOWLES
The French Lieutenant's Woman
JOHN GALSWORTHY
Strife
MRS GASKELL
North and South
WILLIAM GOLDING
Lord of the Flies
The Spire
OLIVER GOLDSMITH
She Stoops to Conquer
The Vicar of Wakefield
ROBERT GRAVES
Goodbye to All That
GRAHAM GREENE
Brighton Rock
The Heart of the Matter
The Power and the Glory
WILLIS HALL
The Long and the Short and the Tall
THOMAS HARDY
Far from the Madding Crowd
Jude the Obscure
Selected Poems
Tess of the D'Urbervilles
The Mayor of Casterbridge
The Return of the Native
The Woodlanders
L. P. HARTLEY
The Go-Between
NATHANIEL HAWTHORNE
The Scarlet Letter
SEAMUS HEANEY
Selected Poems
ERNEST HEMINGWAY
A Farewell to Arms
The Old Man and the Sea
SUSAN HILL
I'm the King of the Castle
BARRY HINES
Kes
HOMER
The Iliad
The Odyssey

GERARD MANLEY HOPKINS
Selected Poems
TED HUGHES
Selected Poems
ALDOUS HUXLEY
Brave New World
HENRIK IBSEN
A Doll's House
HENRY JAMES
The Portrait of a Lady
Washington Square
BEN JONSON
The Alchemist
Volpone
JAMES JOYCE
A Portrait of the Artist as a Young Man
Dubliners
JOHN KEATS
Selected Poems
PHILIP LARKIN
Selected Poems
D. H. LAWRENCE
Selected Short Stories
Sons and Lovers
The Rainbow
Women in Love
HARPER LEE
To Kill a Mocking-Bird
LAURIE LEE
Cider with Rosie
CHRISTOPHER MARLOWE
Doctor Faustus
HERMAN MELVILLE
Moby Dick
THOMAS MIDDLETON *and*
    WILLIAM ROWLEY
The Changeling
ARTHUR MILLER
A View from the Bridge
Death of a Salesman
The Crucible
JOHN MILTON
Paradise Lost I & II
Paradise Lost IV & IX
Selected Poems
V. S. NAIPAUL
A House for Mr Biswas
ROBERT O'BRIEN
Z for Zachariah
SEAN O'CASEY
Juno and the Paycock
GEORGE ORWELL
Animal Farm
Nineteen Eighty-four

JOHN OSBORNE
Look Back in Anger
WILFRED OWEN
Selected Poems
ALAN PATON
Cry, The Beloved Country
THOMAS LOVE PEACOCK
Nightmare Abbey and *Crotchet Castle*
HAROLD PINTER
The Caretaker
SYLVIA PLATH
Selected Works
PLATO
The Republic
ALEXANDER POPE
Selected Poems
J. B. PRIESTLEY
An Inspector Calls
WILLIAM SHAKESPEARE
A Midsummer Night's Dream
Antony and Cleopatra
As You Like It
Coriolanus
Hamlet
Henry IV Part I
Henry IV Part II
Henry V
Julius Caesar
King Lear
Macbeth
Measure for Measure
Much Ado About Nothing
Othello
Richard II
Richard III
Romeo and Juliet
Sonnets
The Merchant of Venice
The Taming of the Shrew
The Tempest
The Winter's Tale
. *Troilus and Cressida*
Twelfth Night
GEORGE BERNARD SHAW
Arms and the Man
Candida
Pygmalion
Saint Joan
The Devil's Disciple
MARY SHELLEY
Frankenstein
PERCY BYSSHE SHELLEY
Selected Poems
RICHARD BRINSLEY SHERIDAN
The Rivals

R. C. SHERRIFF
Journey's End
JOHN STEINBECK
Of Mice and Men
The Grapes of Wrath
The Pearl
LAURENCE STERNE
A Sentimental Journey
Tristram Shandy
TOM STOPPARD
Professional Foul
Rosencrantz and Guildenstern are Dead
JONATHAN SWIFT
Gulliver's Travels
JOHN MILLINGTON SYNGE
The Playboy of the Western World
TENNYSON
Selected Poems
W. M. THACKERAY
Vanity Fair
J. R. R. TOLKIEN
The Hobbit
MARK TWAIN
Huckleberry Finn
Tom Sawyer
VIRGIL
The Aeneid
ALICE WALKER
The Color Purple
KEITH WATERHOUSE
Billy Liar
EVELYN WAUGH
Decline and Fall
JOHN WEBSTER
The Duchess of Malfi
OSCAR WILDE
The Importance of Being Earnest
THORNTON WILDER
Our Town
TENNESSEE WILLIAMS
The Glass Menagerie
VIRGINIA WOOLF
Mrs Dalloway
To the Lighthouse
WILLIAM WORDSWORTH
Selected Poems
WILLIAM WYCHERLEY
The Country Wife
W. B. YEATS
Selected Poems